MILLION DOLLAR MINDSET PRESENTS

MASTERMIND

7 WAYS TO GET INTO THE BIG LEAGUE

by LINKED IN AND TOWN HALL ACHIEVER OF THE YEAR
EY NOMINEE ENTREPRENEUR OF THE YEAR
GRAND HOMAGE LYS DIVERSITY

Dr. BAK NGUYEN, DMD

& Co-Author
JONAS DIOP, BUSINESS COACH

TO ALL OF THOSE DREAMING OF TELLING A STORY, THIS IS
YOUR MOMENT TO SEIZE, YOUR VOICE TO EMPOWER,
YOUR PRESENCE TO NOTICE.

by Dr. BAK NGUYEN
& JONAS DIOP

ISBN: 978-1-989536-26-1

MILLION DOLLAR MINDSET PRESENTS

MASTERMIND

7 WAYS TO GET INTO THE BIG LEAGUE

by Dr. BAK NGUYEN & JONAS DIOP

INTRODUCTION
BY Dr. BAK NGUYEN

INTRODUCTION
BY JONAS DIOP

WHAT'S YOUR DEFINITION OF A BIG LEAGUE AND HOW DO YOU FIND YOUR MOTIVATION?
CHAPTER 1- Dr. BAK NGUYEN

THE STRIVER'S ATTITUDE
CHAPTER 2 - JONAS DIOP

WHAT ARE YOU AIMING FOR?
CHAPTER 3 - Dr. BAK NGUYEN

SHOW WHO YOU ARE
CHAPTER 4 - JONAS DIOP

WHO ARE YOU LOOKING TO CONNECT WITH TO IMPROVE YOURSELF?
CHAPTER 5 - Dr. BAK NGUYEN

THE TRUE ACCEPTANCE
CHAPTER 6 - JONAS DIOP

DO YOU AGREE WITH THE THEORY OF WORK/LIFE BALANCE?
CHAPTER 7 - Dr. BAK NGUYEN

THE HARMONY
CHAPTER 8- JONAS DIOP

HOW DO YOU RECOGNIZE OPPORTUNITIES?
CHAPTER 9 - Dr. BAK NGUYEN

ALWAYS THE HEART FIRST
CHAPTER 10 - JONAS DIOP

HOW DO YOU CREATE LEVERAGE?
CHAPTER 11 - Dr. BAK NGUYEN

REWRITING THE RULES
CHAPTER 12 - JONAS DIOP

WHAT DO YOU WHAT TO LEAVE AS LEGACY?
CHAPTER 13 - Dr. BAK NGUYEN

A KISS FROM A ROSE
CHAPTER 14 - JONAS DIOP

CONCLUSION
BY Dr. BAK NGUYEN

INTRODUCTION

by Dr. BAK NGUYEN

The last time I share with you in this form was a month ago, in the introduction of my 50th book, **HUMILITY FOR SUCCESS**. I won't lie, that was one of the hardest books I had to write to date.

Hard because of the subject, hard because I was exhausted, hard because I was, once again, squeezed in time. And I did it, with a few days before the deadline. Before the end of September, I had completed my new world record, writing **50 books within 25 months**!

A month earlier, I was announcing **48 books within 24 months**. Between two world records, the arrival of the **EAX (Enhanced Audio Book)** on all the major platforms and the advancements of **Mdex & Co**, I was proud of my month.

October started slow... I had a Royal Wedding to attend in Morocco at mid-month and wasn't in a rush to simply rush into another book. Yes, I let the steam down in writing. In the meantime, I wasn't sleeping on my hands either.

My 37th book, **eHappyPedia, The Rise of the Unicorn**, needed my attention after the review of my friend, mentor and co-author, Dr. Jean De Serres. That took a week to review and to rewrite a few chapters.

I always have a harder time to get back into a project and correct or rewrite than to just move forward, jumping headfirst into a new one. The moral is hard to keep up.

To take a step backward, and to revisit my 37th book took much energy. On top of it, I was running late in the editing and publishing on Amazon of the previous books.

After The Rise of the Unicorn, I pushed to have my 3rd and 48th book published, **LEADERSHIP, PAndora's Box,** and **How to Write a Successful Business Plan** finally were available from Amazon in printed format.
Then, it was time to fly to Morocco. Not yet. In my schedule, I had to shake hands of the prime minister of the province. This was organized by a mutual friend. I had to postpone my flight to meet with the prime minister.

Well, the meeting was canceled within 24 hours notice, state urgencies. I wasn't mad. I was glad! That day, I was supposed to meet with the prime minister and then rush to the airport hoping to catch the last flight oversea.

Within the first 10 days of October, I may not have written any new book, but I managed to finish the revision of a book and published two new ones on Amazon. But why did it feel like I was sitting on my hands?

That last day off, out of circumstance, I took a free day to go shopping. I went shopping, took my time and arrive earlier at the airport.

Wow, it's been an eternity since I had time to kill. I am almost a little confused about how to act in these kinds of situations… of having free time.
I must say, I am not used to wait… My entire life, I run and run and sleep, only to wake up and run again. The funny thing is, I did not miss slowing down, but not at all.

I went to Morocco and back. I met great people, powerful people. I even end up with a personal invitation to visit the Head Quarter of the United Nations, both in New York and in Geneva.

No, I am not bragging, if anything, I still have a hard time to believe it myself! I stayed genuine, and people loved me for who I was.

"Being genuine is the kindest
of attitude toward ourselves."
Dr. Bak Nguyen

It is now the third week into October, and I haven't written anything serious yet. Last weekend, I just couldn't stand the fact of having any new book to show within this month, so I started writing **THE STORY OF THE CHICKEN NUGGET**, with William as co-author.

We had the story in mind for some time by now. I had the imagery ready also, so it was an easy win, to simply move dive and to write.

The last time that we wrote together was 4 months ago… it took us some time to pick where we left. 5 days later, we were done, and **THE STORY OF THE CHICKEN**

NUGGET was available for download on Apple Books. This was number 51 and the first one in the month of October.

I could push William to translate it in French the next weekend, and we would have our 22nd book together and my 52nd. But it sounds like a cheat.

I was walking around looking for my next title. Everyone in my entourage all thought that I was crazy: "You wrote 51 books already, just enjoy some free time! You surely earned it."

But that's not it. You have no idea how it feels to be running a marathon of sprints, especially when each new sprint is a new world record. I grew addicted. I can simply not stop!

To understand how it felt, that day off I had shopping, I felt useless to my stomach. Then, in Morocco, I became physically sick... just walking around and "enjoying". I was there to share the joy of two of my closest friends, I met great people, but my **Momentum** was bleeding... dry.

> "Momentum is when it becomes easier
> to keep moving forward than to stop."
> Dr. Bak Nguyen

There is a price for everything. I think that this is mine. I have the power of **Speed** and **Momentum**. I embraced those powers, and they pushed me to reach states of performance that I never suspected I could achieve.

And then, that becomes my nature, my baseline. To cut me from that baseline is like cutting myself from breathing. Yes, it is that deeply entrenched in me by now.

I accept it gladly and gracefully. This is what I shared we a good friend and protege, coach Jonas Diop. That is it! This is our book together!
For months now, we were talking about writing a book together, but I was waiting for Jonas to complete his first one first. Now that his first book is in editing, we are free to start our book.

The title, **MASTERMIND**, we had for a while by now, but the subject was still vague. Jonas looked me in the eye and said that the subject is exactly what I am living at this moment: how am I living and feeding my mindset!

We sat down within an afternoon (again, it wasn't easy to secure time so we both could sit down together). After a productive meeting, we decided to jump, and we went online announcing our collaboration together, the start of my 52nd book, **MASTERMIND, 7 ways into the big league**.

Jonas is a business coach and a podcaster, asking questions, hard questions, empowerment questions, making sense out of them and putting them into a narrative is his natural strength.

Why not? I needed a second book this month, and I had no other alternative. Let's make it fun, shall we? On a Live, we announced that we are starting a book together and that it will be available by the beginning of next month, November 1st.

Precisely, we had 6 days and a half to write, edit and publish **MASTERMIND, 7 ways into the big league**. Jonas gave me a list of questions that I will answer.

He gave me a dozen questions, all based on his insight of me and of being a coach. The purpose of the exercise is to understand the way I process emotions and motivation, mindset, and skill to keep overachieving and delivering.

We shock on it, with our public from facebook as a witness. Today is day one. This shall be very interesting. 7 chapters each, plus introduction and conclusion, and less than a week to deliver.

I know that I will be delivering, Jonas just boosted my motivation, and together, I step up a frame and structure to deliver a book ready to be download on November 1.

> "The fun and the thrill keep me going,
> especially in the hardest spot."
> Dr. Bak Nguyen

This is mainly how I would have restarted my **Momentum**, having fun sharing with you, and looking at Jonas to catch up on my next chapter.

Whatever your goal is, whatever the time frame you gave yourself, it is always easier with fun and company. And by now, I have done enough to know that where it is easy, I can build **Momentum** from!

This is **MASTERMIND, 7 ways into the big league.** Welcome to **MILLION DOLLAR MINDSET**.

I am what I will, and I'll be what I tried.

Dr. BAK NGUYEN

INTRODUCTION
by JONAS DIOP

Welcome onboard. I know that our title is catchy and that you will pick up this fantastic book to have a different approach to your path of success. I have to warn you, the information within this book will get you nowhere if you do not take action.

The right information + Guided actions = Transformation

Following my first book: **NOW OR NEVER**, this one is for conquerors, high achievers, and all the people with dreams and goals to reach. You, who want to reach your full potential and go to your next step in life, in their business, this book is pure gold for you.

I strongly believe that you can have it all: health, greatness, fulfillment, success, and happiness.

For over two decades, I focused all of my being on discovering **THE ART OF MAKING AN IMPACT**, I have my daily routine to read books, to listen to audios, I took some training, went to multiples masterclasses, see gurus and I even launched my own podcast to interview entrepreneurs, risk-takers, and visionaries. This is my passion and life's mission.

My first real breakthrough on the path of Impact was to discover that great achievers share one common point: they all have a team and an entourage, models, coaches, consultants, and mentors. They follow some universals rules that you don't escape as the law of weightlessness for everybody.

They don't reinvent the **WHEEL OF SUCCESS**. They adapt it to their own needs and requirements to improve themselves, to optimize their processes, to reach their goals. They are looking to leverage their past experiences and, using the wheel to propel themselves further in the future.

I met with the top performers, top coaches, and every time, I noticed that they aren't shy to ask the Universe for the wheel or the pieces of the wheel that they need.

"Ask, and you shall receive."

So the first tray of success is to have the humility to recognize what we are missing and to ask for help.

If you need one million dollars, ask one million people a dollar, maybe two... You want to lose weight, reach out for those people in great shape, what are they eating, how they exercise. You'll be surprised how easy it may be to seek answers if you ask the right questions.

"If you want something, anything in life,
ask someone who already processed
what you are looking for."
Jonas Diop

Two years ago, I met this gentleman. I got introduced to him by a common friend. I heard a lot about him. Many people were telling his success story, of how he empowers others to reach their full potential, and how he is bold and overachieving.

I was intrigued, but I wanted the real story. I wanted to know about the real stuff, the story of his failures, grinding, and hardship.

I interviewed him on my podcast, **#DUC - DEVIENS UN CONQUÉRANT**, my goal was to squeeze out of him, his secrets, his tools to power, his skills to success, all patterns of his mindset.

Dr. Bak is very different than the other high achievers that I have the privilege to meet and interviewed. Within the first minutes of our interview, I realize that his focus was not to be in the big league (he already reached such level), but he strives for the impact league.

Like Steve Jobs, Ellon Musk, or the Wright Brothers, he has a dream: **To change the world from a dental chair**, this is also the title of one of his books. Today, he has a breathtaking record of 52 books in 26 months.

I asked him to share his secrets, how to create **Momentum**. I had this goal to write a book about success. I had all the ideas but no manuscript.

Well, Dr. Bak helped me with kindness to start and finish my first book.

Hustle respects hustle. We are achievers. Through this journey, we became friends and brothers. We became allies.

I watch him pull people, institutions and the Universe to raise **Mdex & Co**, the company that he co-founded with partner and wife, Tranie Vo. **Mdex & Co** is the most innovative project in the field of dentistry in North America. I was on the first row, looking at a man building his empire and legacy.

This is simply too great and too tempting as a temptation. I always wanted to be involved in this kind of vision, in a project of this scope, to change the world, nothing less! So I reached out, I asked.

Today, I am one of his lieutenant, one that he trusts, and has fun with as we expand his vision to empower the world for the better. His answer is the philosophy behind **Mdex & Co**.

Let's come back to **WHY** of this book. Like King Salomon, I ask for wisdom when I am challenged, I truly believe that's a gift. I look for the opportunity to outgrow myself, to pay attention to the impact.

Thursday, October 24th, 2019, Dr. Bak challenged me to co-write a book about success with him.

I was thrilled. I was waiting for the opportunity for many months by now. But there was a little catch. We have to do it within a week. We literally had less than 7 days to write, edit and publish a book on Apple Books. That's not all, the book will be written in English.

Do I have to tell you that I speak French? I can find my way in English, speaking. But writing… a book?! English is not my first language, and this is my second book…

But coming from Dr. Bak, my friend and mentor, I couldn't refuse the opportunity nor the challenge. I will give it my best!

To seal the deal, we went **LIVE** online and announced to the world the beginning of the writing of **MASTERMIND, 7 WAYS INTO THE BIG LEAGUE,** and that it will be available for download by November 1st, 2019. The heat was on.

We agreed on the structure of the book. When it comes to writing books, he is the expert and the veteran.

When it comes to interviews, I was the big fish in the water. I gave Dr. Bak a list of questions about his mindset, definitions of life, skills and meaning that would squeeze out of him the **JUICE OF SUCCESS**.

I want more than the success story, I want the real grind, the real talk, the real Life so I could draw parallels with the crowd and other great minds.

Are you ready for a journey of empowerment? Are you hungry for success? Together, we will learn from a super overachiever, not by copying him, but by breaking down his thought process and reverse engineering his mindset.

Are you ready to step foot in the **Impact league**? Do you want to transcend yourself and to go to the next level? I summon the Genie from Aladdin, I already rub the lamp for you.

This is **MASTERMIND, 7 ways into the big league.** Welcome to **MILLION DOLLAR MINDSET**.

One decision can turn your life around,
and you just need to take it.

JONAS DIOP

CHAPTER 1

"WHAT'S YOUR DEFINITION OF A BIG LEAGUE AND HOW DO YOU FIND YOUR MOTIVATION?"

by Dr. BAK NGUYEN

Actually, until I started writing this book, I never thought about the big league. Big, small, those are unimportant to me. I am not saying that to look good. Really, I do not care much about the labels.

All of my life, before I attended dental school, I was bread among the elite. Never it was enough, never it was good. If I had 90%, why didn't I had 95% or 100%? If I had 100%, get over it, and concentrate on the next one!

Don't even think about coming back home, showing 70%! Don't even care to show your face home! Sure, I am exaggerating a little, but not by too much.

I attended a private college for High School, College Jean-Eudes, which, I am told, is one of the best in the city. There too, it was never enough. I had much fun, though.

So over time, I learned to leverage my ability to perform at school and to deliver the most with as little investment as possible.

To me, if I can get 85% putting in only an hour studying, that was a good deal. What about the other 15%? Well, those will require another 4 hours…

> "4 hours for 15% versus 1 hour for 85%,
> the deal is pretty clear to me."
> Dr. Bak Nguyen

Despite my laziness and tendency to cut corners, I am still a perfectionist. Maybe, that's what saved me. In my line of duty as a dental surgeon, results are everything! And the result is not just what you see, it is how you feel.

So I learned to connect genuinely with my patients and the people I deal with. I know what I can deliver, will make it look good, but above all, I will make sure that they feel good about themselves looking at it.

So what does this have to do with my definition of a big league? I just shared with you my process. Today, I am a big league dentist. I never noticed when I got there, but the success was hard to deny.

I was propelled there because I was concentrating on my delivering, not the status. Actually, I was only aware of my status the day I started writing books to share my experience. Once again, because I aimed at the sharing part, the status was merely a side effect.

I wrote my first book and my second. Today, this one is my 52nd book, within 26 months! I am in the big league! AM I? What would that change to my life? Absolutely nothing!

I started writing books to get prepared to hit the stage. Then, I discover a talent sharing with words and emotions. I kept writing because it felt good and because I loved what and who I was becoming.

I focused on the fun, and today, every new title I write is a new world record. So I guess, if you want to learn from me, don't care much about the status nor the labeling.

Big league, small league, major or minor, those are words people use to position you. To me, the only position I see is how far am I from my next victory.

I would love to tell you that all I have are victories, but the most part of my life, I dealt with failures. Actually, to be fair, I have a selective memory that will remember more the failures than the victories.

The reason is simple, every time I win, I am happy, sure, but I am also moving on to the next one, leaving it a small imprint on my mind.

Now, each time that I fail, trust me, the emotions run much deeper, and I will be obsessed with writing my wrongs. In other words, I won't stop until I have come back on the table with a win.

In my perspective of things, I spend much more time bathing and chewing my failures than my successes. And since I am a positive person, imagine the effect that it does to my morals, to chew day in and day out, my failures?!

To cope with such, I just threw away the labels. I chew, I think, I do. Some things will take longer, and some will be faster. I will be there until it is done.

So to truly answer the question, I don't know much about the big league, I have no control over the league, and whatever I can't change, I don't care! You read right, I simply don't care!

"Only care about the things you can change. The rest are extra burdens that you don't need."
Dr. Bak Nguyen

What I know, though, is to score. Wherever you are, whatever the size and the impact of your game, do it with all of your heart and to it to matter.

If today, I am interviewed by coach Jonas Diop about big league and mindset, it is thanks to the impact my results have over his perception.

So whatever you do, do it right and do it until the end! That brings us to our next question, what is the end or to what end?

To define a goal is very important. In any kind of game, the rules, the goal, and the time limit are what will define a winner from a loser. It is the same in real life and entrepreneurship.

You must define the rules, the goal, and the time frame. Sure, you can stretch the boundaries for a certain time, but without ground rules, it is impossible to know a defeat from a victory.

The worse that you can do is to rationalize and postpone the final score indefinitely.

"Some times, it is better to record a loss,
and to digest it, than to keep the books open,
and not deal with the loss."
Dr. Bak Nguyen

Just like any of you, I hate to lose. Can I be any clearer? But at the same time, I know that lose, and failures are part of the game, so I cheat by removing the label, and I chew all of them up until I find a way to leverage them.

Yes, a loss is a liability. It is also the opportunity to grow and to come back bigger, stronger, smarter.

That's why you should record that loss and start dealing with it.

> "Every time I win, I am happy.
> Every time I lose, I am motivated."
> Dr. Bak Nguyen

Sure, it is not fun to lose, but would you really close the door to an invitation to evolve? In business, the common wisdom will tell you to suppress your emotions. Emotions are usually bad for business…

Not necessary. Playing that game of win/loss, use the deception and frustration of a loss to propel your evolution. Think about it. It is never easy nor fun to change the way we are.

In front of a loss, we have no choice but to change our old ways. Leveraging on your emotions was the easiest way to evolve without too much resistance, at least from yourself.

In the same line of logic, aim for the next win. No matter small or big, feed yourself on that win. You will feel different, taller and lighter.

Use those same emotions to jump back in the game as soon as possible to go each your next win. This is mainly how I managed to build and entertain my superpower, my **Momentum**.

"To build Momentum, build upon each win,
as quickly as possible. If you need to replenish,
do it while running."
Dr. Bak Nguyen

Keeping score and playing the game of win/loss, I just shared with you how to leverage our emotions, good and bad, to keep moving forward and to cut on procrastination.

On the subject of procrastination, I learned that the longer I stand on a win, the bigger the temptation for **Pride** and **Ego**. The longer I stand on a loss, the higher the psychological wall and the doubt.

So the answer was pretty simple to me: whatever win or loss, I move forward without procrastination and bringing with me only the necessary burden: no drama, no regrets, no pain, just the experience that I can leverage on to get to the next stage.

On that, the rules are crucial to me. Before I enter any game, I must know the rules, even if I might break them or rewrite them, I must know the goal, my goal, but above all, I must know the time frame, even if I might bend it.

This is how I keep myself motivated by moving forward, light-weighted and with **speed** and **Momentum**. Labels, expectations, doubts, status are all burdens that I have a hard time leveraging on. That is why I strongly advise all of you to simply discard them, along with your past medals.

You heard right, even your past medals are unnecessary burdens that will slow you down on the path of your next win.

Is this the big league? I'll let you be the judge. If this is the big league, what will come next? Seriously, none of those answers can serve as leverage to me. So here is my genuine answer: I don't know, and I couldn't care less.

I will keep moving forward, feeding on y wins, and leveraging on my failures. I will move forward following the path of my next win. Win or loss, I will move quickly not to grow roots, doubts, or pride. I will rest will running or flying. I will enjoy what is ahead.

"There is no life in the past, just death, and souvenirs."
Dr. Bak Nguyen

This is my life and my shoot at Life. I am what I will, and I'll be what I tried.

This is **MASTERMIND, 7 ways into the big league.** Welcome to **MILLION DOLLAR MINDSET**.

I am what I will, and I'll be what I tried.
Dr. BAK NGUYEN

CHAPTER 2

"THE STRIVER'S ATTITUDE"

by JONAS DIOP

I started my journey to learn about success because I saw my mom working so hard to raise her 4 children by herself. She was a brilliant entrepreneur, at the age of 28 years old, she owned 3 hair saloons and one perfumery.

Her fortune turned in by the end of the '80s when she had to shut down all of her commerces, one after one due to the recession.

I remembered seeing my mom, at the age of 3 years old, coming home late at night, way after the sun has set. And then, every time I woke up, she was already cutting hair. She worked hard and passed on those values to me.

I know that working hard will pay off, but do we really to endure all the challenges? The answer is simple, we are conditioned, conditioned to believe that working hard will deliver results, we are strivers.

"We capitalize too much on effort, not cleverness."
Jonas Diop

We capitalize on closing the gap between our weaknesses and our strengths. The school system taught us to be balanced, but in real life, you need to be unbalanced to move forward.

I see successful people have all that I look for: stability, comfort, health, wealth, etc… I don't know all their stories, but I am pretty sure that they don't work harder than my mom. I, myself, am a grinder, too, and you know what Dr. Bak once told me? That I work too hard for my money. Coming from a man who literally never stops, I took the advice to heart. We have to choose our battles.

In the world of martial arts, one has to choose a specialty to master. You choose your weapon, your style, you focus on one discipline, and then, you train until you have mastered the art.

To reach the pinnacle of it and to enlighten your potential, you must be dedicated and remained focus, not balanced.

I am not surprised by Dr. Bak's answer. High achievers capitalize on their strengths, they see the world differently without much ego. They know their talents and are aware of their limits. They master the art of focusing.

What I learned from one of my mentors, Grant Cardone, is to be **obsessed**. To succeed, you must have an addiction to greatness. Don't overreact, we all have an addiction for something, for some, it is cigarettes, others, alcohol. Well, for the high and overachievers, it is their goal.

Grant is deploring the fact that our society has a heavy tendency to label people quickly with tags as ADHD, ADD, workaholic, and many more. If you are listening to them, everyone who has any potential to rise above the crowd is having a condition of some sort, and the names always sounded as an illness.

If you look at the high achievers, many, if not all of them have those kinds of labels. They do not try to fill out the hole, they are just trying to reach their full potential.

Looking at them, you can see that all of them are too busy running that they are hardly affected by the label… Those affected are those staying behind and watching them rise, those who were once close to.

Never compare yourself to anyone. You are special, you are unique. That's it. You must accept and embrace who you are. Only then, can you compete with yourself, for yourself? You do so to be your **best version**.

You can create a Momentum by action, by decision. Some are great, some will lead to disappointment. As Dr.Bak said, you win or you learn.

Remember your worst failure, and that is your greatest lesson. Focus on building from your ashes, like a forest after a fire, step by step, tree buds after tree buds. No one can build a castle on his/her first day.

Dr. Bak always told me: we are all born winners, we simply need to believe it. You win the race of Life. This book is not only about sharing tips, secrets or principles but this book is also about empowering yourself.

You already know the law of Pareto: 80/20, 20% of what you do, will deliver 80% of the results. You already know the information, but you need to experiment. You need to have some proof to overcome your doubts, and to strengthen your faith.

"We all have issues, insecurities, but we also have dreams. Unfortunately, we have pride too."
Jonas Diop

Our motivation does not need to originate from fears. Facing fear, we have 3 options:

- **Be paralyzed.** This happened within this journey with Dr. Bak, as he sent me his chapters by email, one after the next, several times in the same day. I froze.
- **Runaway**, but that wasn't an option anymore since I went online and announced to the world that I would finish this book in a week. Fleeing was out of the table.
- **Attack**. That's was the only choice left for me to choose from. I put myself to the task, and I gave it my best. I did so just as if I was fighting for my life.

I choose not to be motivated by fear, but by love, to share the knowledge that can help, to share experiences. Right now, I am delivering my love to you through those lines. Can you feel the love?

We are not looking for the big league, we are looking for the **impact**.

Dr. Bak follows the same path of all of the high achievers before him: he is not giving a dime about labels, he is focused on doing his thing, those that he judges meaningful, he is dedicated to leave a legacy, to change the world from a dental chair!

He's taking the challenge to play the big game of life with an **ALL-IN** attitude. He is laser-focused on his vision and makes it big like Grant Cardone.

You, too, can do it. It is not a matter of potential, but one of awareness and of choice, we were all born winner, remember? You can reach your full potential by saying to yourself: you are destined to succeed. Do so, cleverly.

This is **MASTERMIND, 7 ways into the big league.** Welcome to **MILLION DOLLAR MINDSET**.

One decision can turn your life around, you just need to take it.

JONAS DIOP

CHAPTER 3

"WHAT ARE YOU AIMING FOR?"

by Dr. BAK NGUYEN

This is an excellent and very interesting question. I started just like any of you, looking for a way to find myself and to prove myself. Over time, I learned to accept what and who I was to let myself be and to discover where it would lead.

"I am no smarter, just learning on the way. I do walk and run every day, though."
Dr. Bak Nguyen

This is how I learned to see the world differently. We are all trained to understand the means and importance of money and power.

POWER

Let's face it, power we started with none. Every time we had power, it was more a responsibility than anything else. Then, we realized that power is just that, a responsibility. Is it fun? Not at all.

"In financial vocabulary,
power is mainly a big liability!"
Dr. Bak Nguyen

We will come back on the subject later, but let say that power wasn't what I was aiming for, despite the appearance. Just to make it clear, I was looking to keep my freedom of movement and action, that I did.

The real power I was looking up to was and still is to the power over myself. That, I learned to never, but never relinquish. Not to my love, not to my kids, not to my parents, not to my friends, not to my mentors, not to my professors, not to society and especially not to religion or any doctrine.

I am my own mind. I am open to listen, I will be respectful, but I am making my own choice and will bear their consequences. This is the only power that I have and the only power that I believe in, the power over myself.

MONEY

Then, there is money. One can buy pretty much everything with money, right? Wait before you answer this one. The obvious and by default answer is, absolutely not... but within a journey of 42 years, I've come to see that not much is out of reach of money since money can buy time!

In our modern societies, we have built up all of our social ladder upon who's better, smarter, stronger. But all of those are hard to prove unless one gets naked and into an arena to prove his/her point. As a collective, we have grown much lazier and to prove ourselves is often too much of an effort.

Instead, we will talk and show our attributes. Sadly enough, most of the time, this is sufficient to convince the other of our point. Talk is cheap, but it is a better bargain to the actual fight and walks. Are we that dumb? Not completely.

We are impressible. The show of force is amplified with people, followers, gears, and fanfare. In other words, attributes that money can buy. The worse part is when we are attracted to join in… we too were for sale!!!

That's the power of money if one has no power over him/herself. It is not wrong, just a choice, but a choice that we should be aware of, and not to be taken lightly.

And in today's society, money, we all have. Maybe not as much as you wish we had, but we do have some. Is it power? Does it feel good? I'll let you have a minute to whisper your answer.

Yup, you are right. Money is not what we thought. It is a powerful mean, but one that can corrupt its master into a slave. Even though I need money. I need money to buy Time!

TIME

Yup, Time, the most important resource that I hold. But not in the sense that you think. Time is useless to me if I can't leverage it.

Just like any of you, I wake up I'm the morning fresh and with twenty-some hours in front of me. For the first minutes of the day, I am the master of that **gift of freedom and opportunity**.

But soon enough, the routine of life takes over, and I am going, just like any of you, with the flow. It is not wrong, just pointless.

Younger, I woke up to go to school. Then, I woke up to go to looking for a job, I didn't find one that suited me, so I woke up to built my job. Today, I woke up every day to keep that job going... Does this make any sense to you?

And I am very grateful for my life. I've spent countless hours, days and years to build what I today call my daily. But this can't be it. I should wake up to get laid, that will make more sense!

So I fix the problem differently: I will never go to sleep anymore! You read right, this is where the difference is made. I decided to stay awaken all the time… until exhaustion hits me and I drop dead, 10, 12 hours later.

I did not go to sleep, I dropped dead. If this is it, well, I did my part. But until now, 6 hours later, I am back up on my feet, fully awaken.

This is how I started writing, waking up earlier 1 or 2 hours before sunrise. Those minutes are precious since they are all mine before society and routine take over.

Because I wake up fully aware, I don't have to "start" my day, I simply have to resume what I left unfinished a few hours ago. But also, that pause allowed me to sort things out and to see everything with more clarity.

Within months, what I can write and produce within those two before dawn hours were mainly the most valuable productivity of my days. One hour became two, and, slowly, it took over my the entirety of the realm of the day.

I was productive because I felt free. I didn't have to count the minutes nor to rush into the next thing scheduled. So I gave in to the feeling of **ABUNDANCE** and of **FREEDOM**, and simply enjoy discovering what my mind could do.

Chapter by chapter, a book was completed. Book after book, I started a library and accumulating world records to be recognized, but I've done it, that no one can take away... and frankly, I do not care much, I know what I am worth.

The beauty and magic touched another level the day my son of 7 wanted to join in. William started writing books with me, and it simply defined all the laws of arithmetic. From **15 books/15 months**, we scored **8 children books/1 month.** Only to keep going.

By my 18th month + 1 week of writing, I had 36 books to show for, adults (15k - 46k words/book) and children (more or less 5-6k words plus images). I don't know about you, but this is not time efficiency nor time management. This is **freedom** and **inspiration**. It is **passion** and **love**.

Well, today, it is my **POWER**, the power to bend time, and the power to define the laws of arithmetic. What started with an hour or two at the beginning of the day now is the frame of my days and nights.

How to do so is a long, very long story. For those of you who are interested, my 7th book, **MOMENTUM TRANSFER,** written with coach Dino Masson, is covering the essential step to create a **Momentum** and to **leverage emotions** into Time.

"To live forever or to be forever young, which is best?"
Dr. Bak Nguyen

From the beginning of time, we have those stories and legends about the secret of eternal life. Then, the stories slowly morphed into the fountain of youth. If we do not pay attention, the story is the same. Actually, one is a curse and the other one, well, I haven't decided yet what it is.

When we stop and think on the matter, it's not about being there forever, but about being happy that we are all looking for. We have the false belief that if we are happy, we should freeze time at that exact moment. This is what it meant to live forever.

Well, the curse happened when everyone else dies around us. To continue alone now became a curse instead of a blessing.

Others will like the abundance of Eternity to live their lives and dream. But once one has all Eternity to achieve something, in other words, playing a game that has no time limits, can you see the problem? There is no Momentum, no fun and then, no real reward.

And this is assuming that all that time, Eternity also provides young and health and invulnerability. What if one is cripple, will he/she stay that way for Eternity too? This will be an interesting subject to explore.

This is how I understood that **Time** alone is not what to aim for either.

ENERGY

So I went for Energy instead. Energy is Life, and Energy is what gave me my superpower, **Speed** and **Momentum**. Just like Life itself, Energy can present itself under many forms, some completely different than the other, some, even opposite.

And every time you put two energies together, some always happen. An explosion, a fight, a synergy, an annihilation, whatever it is, something happens.

$$\text{ENERGY} \varpropto \frac{\text{DESIRE} \cdot \text{WILL}}{\text{VALUES}}$$

So I went out looking for a formula of Energy that I can harness and leverage on. That is what I arrived with: that Energy is proportional to our desire exponential our will to act on it, the whole, divide by our values (identity).

- In other words, if one has no **desire**, one has no energy.
- One can **multiple exponential** his/her desire with his/her will to act on it, resulting in much, much Energy available.
- And one can harness such Energy at its full potential only when he/she is really **selfless** (a minimum imprint of identity and values).

You should sleep on the formula and its philosophy for some time until it makes sense to you, completely and naturally.

But this is what I look forward to what I aim at, to raise my level of Energy. With Energy, I feel alive, young, and in power. With Energy, I feel that nothing is out of reach, nor impossible.

Can I be any clearer? With **Energy**, I attract. So from Energy, I derive my **creativity**, my **enthusiasm,** and I create. People gathered around and bought. I have money.

From the gathering around me, I leverage and attract more people. Some just bought what I have created, others wanted more, they wanted to do the same thing. So I showed them.

Soon enough, I had a team delivering my creation. That's how I leverage on **Time**. Now, I have more time at my disposal.

Then, I interact and connect with each individual gathering around me. Over time, I became a **center of attraction**. With some, the interaction was minimal. With most, it was productive.

But with a few special people I met, we created **SYNERGY** out of our encounter. This is how I could redraft the world and make it better. This is how I could write as much and still have something new to say, it is out of the **SYNERGY of my journey**.

Since **SYNERGY** is from the encounters of my journey, mostly people, but also events and titans, it is sourcing from what I felt in those presences and how I choose to react to them. In two words, **feelings, emotions**.

You wanted my secret, here it is: **EMOTIONS**. Learn to channel your emotions, to understand, and to ride them, and you will find your way to great powers, yours!

Just like **Energy** will manifest under many different forms and shapes, I don't think that the equation I gave you is the unique equation for Energy, but one of the ways to it. I found my powers from that path, even if I wasn't fully aware of it.

So first, define your **desires**. It is okay if you change them over time, but to work, the desire must be yours. Then, work on your **willpower** and your determination to make it happen.

You don't have to know what to do, you just have to want to make it happen and be open to learn and adapt.

And then comes the hard part. You will have to find out about yourself, to find your **identity**. Once you know and have fully accepted who and what you are, you will grow in confidence.

Only when you will have grown confident enough, can you forget about yourself, your doubts, your limitations, and the burden of your legacy to release the **Energy** you have harness inside?

"One legend can only begin once
one's quest of identity is over."
Dr. Bak Nguyen

With this, you are fully equipped to find your own way, your Destiny. I think that this is really what I am looking for, to walk my Destiny, fully.

Many will say to die without regret, others will sing; they did it their way. Listen to the conviction, feel the inspiration and follow that voice in you.

"Whatever you were seeking,
you will always find it inside."
Dr. Bak Nguyen

This is **MASTERMIND, 7 ways into the big league.** Welcome to **MILLION DOLLAR MINDSET**.

I am what I will, and I'll be what I tried.
Dr. BAK NGUYEN

CHAPTER 4
"SHOW WHO YOU ARE"
by JONAS DIOP

Little, I was shy and introvert. I did not want to make any waves of any kind. I had no ideal, almost no ambition. By the age of 15, everything took a turn for the better.

I started reading tons and tons of books, and I became heavily invested in the success and how to achieve great things. I invested all of my being in self-improvement. I read and learn from masters and great minds, all high achievers in their time and from any standard, past and present.

All share the same keys: to have a **WHY** and to have a clear vision of what they want. I rapidly learned to have **S.M.A.R.T objectives**:

S: SPECIFIC
M: MEASURABLE
A: ACHIEVABLE
R: REALISTIC
T: TIME BOUND

One of my friend Bakate Ba told me that to have a **WHY** is not enough, we need to have a **BECAUSE** since a **BECAUSE** is much deeper than a **WHY**. A **BECAUSE** involves a cause that is bigger than you, it is bigger than just hitting a target. A **BECAUSE** is a journey of possibilities, it is an ideal.

Dr. Bak hit me again with his unfiltered answer, no lies, no trick, just core and purity.

Everyone looking for power, are in fact, filling their insecurities. They are insecure, so they feel the need to control our destinies, not just theirs. Let me define what power is: **POWER** is the ability to create movement, to gain control.

Money isn't the root of evil or all sins, it just reveals who you really are. It allows to make your **impact** bigger. If you are generous, you will be more generous, if you are mad, you will become worst.

Successful people are seeking wealth as a mean and not as an end, a mean to accomplish greater things, to reach something bigger than themselves.

Many talk about giving back. To give back what's they've received. On that point, Dr. Bak has a very original way to present his giving back, tricking and trading his fear for motivation. Very, very ingenious and clever, I must add.

I repeat again, I strongly believe that we can have it all: wealth, health, fulfillment, success, recognition, freedom. I must ask to receive, then, we must deliver on what we've received.

Dr. Bak nailed this concept perfectly with **Energy** and **Synergy**. From quantum physics, we've learned that everything is energy. Our body is a field of energy moving in another field of energy that is the universe. In that line of thoughts we are all connected, so why not make it a better place, the world, the universe?

I like to believe that humans are born with a natural instinct that we are all seeking peace, freedom and safety. We are born to express ourselves, to impact this world. Are you willing to do so? Yes, of course, you want to be respected, you want to care, and to taste **LIFE**.

The bottom line of all of our actions, decisions, sacrifice, we are looking for emotions, we are looking to be happy. Surprised? The quest of our entire life is to find happiness and to stay in that state of mind, in that state of energy.

"Karma is not a bitch, Karma is a blessing."
Jonas Diop

The more energy you give, the more you move, the more you move you, the more Energy you'll generate. That's the **equation of Abundance!**

One of my role models is Sir Richard Branson, the founder of Virgin. The slogan of the Virgin group is **The culture of pleasure**. In other words, to cultivate **PLEASURE**. What a great place to hang out!

His mantra is to live to have rewarding experiences. He was built his life and wealth on those terms. We all saw him enjoying a healthy lifestyle with his jet traveling the world.

Right now, besides to do the channel crossing in Kite Surf at the age of 61 years, besides to do car racing championship, 50% of his time is allowed to develop non-profits organizations to make an **impact.** Like Dr. Bak says, you need to have the **trinity**: **Time, Power, Money** to make a difference in people's life.

At the end of your journey on this earth, you will face two choices:

- One is to be **proud** of yourself
- The second one is to **regret**

Well, Dr. Bak does not live on regrets. He keeps moving forward to generate more energy. This is what he calls his **Momentum**, always going faster and faster.

Sir William Branson and Dr. Bak both have the power to bend realities because they keep moving, generating more **Energy**. With Energy, they are attracting **MONEY** and **POWER**.

Well, from there, the equation is simpler. They use the **MONEY** to leverage **POWER** and doing so they are buying **TIME**. By leveraging power, I meant they have the **INFLUENCE** to move things… which is the definition of POWER itself.

Can you now see clearly the mechanism:

MOVEMENT generates **ENERGY**.
ENERGY attract **MONEY**.
MONEY and **ENERGY** influence **POWER**.
And **MONEY** can buy **TIME**.
With more **TIME**, they can then
Create more **ENERGY**.

The key here is **ENERGY**. **MONEY** is just a commodity and a token to realize vision and purpose.

To have **MONEY**, you need to focus on **ENERGY**. To having more **ENERGY**, you need **TIME** bought with **MONEY**. Moving forward is the best way to generate **ENERGY,** and from there, you are starting to walk the **Path of Abundance**.

Send your notice to the whole entire world, you are coming to express yourself, to taste all of Life. Are you willing to live in the happiness state forever? Of course, you are!

This is **MASTERMIND, 7 ways into the big league.** Welcome to **MILLION DOLLAR MINDSET**.

One decision can turn your life around, you just need to take it.

JONAS DIOP

CHAPTER 5

"WHO ARE YOU LOOKING TO CONNECT WITH TO IMPROVE YOURSELF?"

by Dr. BAK NGUYEN

This is a very tricky question, it all depends where you are in your own evolution and your journey of awareness. Many times over, I told you that your legend could only begin the day you are out of your **Quest of Identity**. Well, that is step one.

THE QUEST OF IDENTITY

Growing up with your parents, with your siblings, friends and school, you were given a name. Then, you had your preference and your surrounding gave you a personality.

Yes, they gave you a personality, since everything they like, they will reinforce and everything they dislike, they will force you to amputate.

The images might be extreme, but it is literally what is happening on an energy and psychological level. We've all been through such process, in the name of love, they will forge us from the fire of conformity. Why do you think that so many of us hated school?

School was just part of the picture. Family, legacy, peer pressure, religion all contribute to put more and more layer to shape our views, opinions and definition of reality.

So, we've spent the first part of our lives connecting, and this what happened. They will give us money, opportunity, love, even time. In the process, we gave up our energy.

Sooner or later, we will wake up in a shiny armor built from the layer of burn and licensing of conformity. We will be functional, many even powerful, but we are walking around with our prison and cast on our shoulders.

To break free from that one, no one can really help us. A wild spirit, a much more experienced one, can wake us up. Most of the time, it is an event that will throw us senseless through the wall that will awake us up.

Sooner or later, the cracks will start showing throw the shiny armor. Blood and the smell of burnt flesh will emerge from the cracks. You can either panic and close up the crack with another layer of conformity, one a little thicker, one a little heavier.

Or you can decide to remove that piece of armor to see what lay underneath. It might stink, it might be disgusting, but it is you, a hurt version of you. Let the light in and expose it to fresh air. You'll be surprised how fast it will start to heal. This is when and where you will be starting your **Quest of Identity**.

You got your shiny armor from listening to others. It is pretty natural not to repeat the same pattern, at least, right away. So you will need to find your support elsewhere.

Books and testimonials of others who've walked the same path are often your only sources of information. You are not looking for guidance nor a how-to protocol, it is **YOUR QUEST of IDENTITY,** remember? All you can have out of those is an inspiration and some pointing in the right direction.

One by one, you will start removing the layer of that shiny armor. Every time you rip a bigger piece, and every time, part of your burning skin goes with the armor. It will be painful, but strangely, it will feel good.

You will be exposed, more and more. Some pieces of armor, you might decide to keep, some others, you wish never to see it again. For the first time since your childhood, you will be looking in the mirror and see who you really are.

For years, the only thing genuine-looking back at you were those eyes, from the reflection of the mirror. Now you can see your shape, your mind, your exaggerations, where you are heavier, and where you are lighter.

Take the time you need to accept and to embrace what you see. It shouldn't be that hard since somewhere, you always felt who you were, you were only deceived by what you saw from the mirror of society.

Until that point, you are better on your own. You might share your bed and your heart with a confident, but once, again, you will only attract what you project. You might not attract someone you will share for long with since you are in the middle of your own mutation process. Really, you are better on your own.

"The Quest of Identity is mostly a lonely path.
Everyone has to walk it, and no one can do
this one with you."
Dr. Bak Nguyen

And then, it gets better. Once you have accepted who and what you are, with the shiny, the steel and the hypocrisy. You are ready to heal.

You will go on to your life, from the outside, you will look the same, but you now start to see everything differently.

Your level of energy is increasing from the decreasing out your values (the shiny armor that you left behind). Whatever was left of you after your awakening is now slowly growing stronger at each breath of air. Enjoy the feeling, there is much for you to do ahead.

Now that you have a taste of the energy from your birthright, it is time for you to find your desires, the real ones. Again, it was not that you do not know what you want, but more a matter to accept it, so you can act on it.

Desires can change faster than you would like. This is where you will need to be open to connect. Not just with the same crowd who forged your previous armor, this time it is time for you to jump in the water and to swim naked with all the people. Be open to touch, to talk, to kiss to experiment.

Until now, others told you what to like and what to hate, what to embrace, and what to hate. Don't you think it is time for you to figure it out on your own? Be open, be respectful and listen to your body.

On the matter, do not trust your head at this stage, since that 10% is the remanent of your time in the forge. Only your heart can serve as a guide in the naked journey.

"Your name was given, now it is time for you
to give it its worth."
Dr. Bak Nguyen

This is how I reset myself and got rid completely of my shiny armor and the remanent of conformity. I am doing it without rebelling, without anger.

If anything, I hold gratitude as the only true feeling, gratitude to my parents, and those who loved and raised me.

They loved me and wanted to protect me to the best of their abilities. They saw the sea, and since they themselves don't know how to swim, leave alone cruise the 7 seas or surf the tallest typhoon, they close the doors, keeping me safe. They did that out of love and fear.

But through the window and kept seeing the wave calling my name. Every time I received a new piece of armor, there was a ceremony and the honor, but always the sea kept calling my name. The doors and gates slowly became what I bear on my shoulder as a sign of prestige and my place in society.

Only my eyes were still free to recognize my name from the sea and the sirens underneath the waves. And I jumped, with the full weight of my armor.

I could have drowned, but I jumped early enough in time to have enough strength to compensate for the weight. In the water, I started ripping away the helmet, the mask, the gauntlets, the boots.

The more I was stripping myself from the shiny, the more people came to me. I was still underwater, and I look up, those like me, those who raised me and those growing by my side, all look from outside the water, with their eyes full of interrogations or judgmental thinking. Whatever happened in their head, they all stood frozen, looking at my drawing underwater.

Only my best friend and wife jump right after me. My little boy followed too. They are not as heavily armored, and the dive was easier for them. This is not love, this is commitment and a genuine desire to stay connected.

Underwater, the feeling is a totally different one. I did not drown, I healed and grew in strength. Those people coming to me, some were sharks, some, pirañas, some red fishes, and some real forces of nature.

Now that I am free to move and to choose, I can rebuild my entourage and surroundings. From the past and those looking down on me, I have to tell you that I keep a good souvenir of our time together, that I understand their pains and doubts and that I am there to help them the day they will be jumping in, but until that day, we will go our separate ways.

"Loyalty is to a cause, not to any individual."
Dr. Bak Nguyen

On that, what about my wife, who faithfully jumped right after me? She is not mine to keep. She is my best friend and deserves my love and respect. She, too, will have to part from her shield and armor.

She jumped in because of me, and I will be by her side for as long as she wants my company. My loyalty to her love is one that I will bear beyond the grave.

That kid who just jumped in the water, following his parents, this is my desire, my desire and determination not to burden him with the same armor and forging process. I will not allow anyone to cut off his wings and to infringe on his confidence and self-love.

He doesn't need pride or ego, he needs space and love and freedom to discover for himself what he loves and what he wants to feed his desires with.

Sure, I had my desires, but looking at my son, I got the certainty of my purpose: to be a great model to him, one without the helmet, the shiny, the pain and the lies.

All parents want their kids to be happy, smart and strong. By the time we are talking about strong, we have long forgotten the happy part. I won't do that.

I will be looking for my own happiness, so I know what I am talking about. He will just have to decide if he wants to follow or not.

I will protect him but preparing him. I will protect him but knowing the way first. So everything I wish for him, I walk the path first. And then, it will be for him to choose to follow or not.

He jumped headfirst in the water, when captains and generals, doctors, and distinguish friend stood there staring. He gave me faith and hope, he showed me the weakness of the lies, despite the shiny and the armor.

$$\text{ENERGY} \propto \frac{\text{WILL} \cdot \text{DESIRE}}{\text{VALUES}}$$

So my Energy went up because I got rid of most of my values. When my son followed in, my determination and willpower were strength looking at him. His was the materialization of the love I shared for now nearly 20 years, so my will increase drastically.

That, in itself, will have sufficed to increase my Energy exponentially. But why stop there? I sill can work on the desired part? This is now for me to choose what I wish to empower.

This is how meeting and genuinely connecting with many people, people from different shores, from different ages, from different cultures, feed my desires.

"To be open was one of my biggest success
in my journey. It brought power, fun,
and legendary to the table."
Dr. Bak Nguyen

The attract who we are and what we have to offer. Among the people I met with, some are from another caliber, another level. Those people I call mentors.

MENTORS

Mentors are people like you, sharing the same kind of path and of discovering, but they made the journey once or twice already. They look at you and recognize a younger version of themselves. That is what attracted them to you.

Welcome their presence. Offer them your gifts, Time. You have youth and energy to offer. They have experience and wisdom. Always be respectful and grateful, but never forget that you are looking for inspiration to make your own choice, not guidance to forget a new armor. Never relinquish control.

In the journey with your mentors, learn to know who are those you get inspiration from. Listen, be respectful, but do not be blind. They have their own stories of success and failure.

You want to hear those and to learn from the experience, but do not try to replicate their story. This is will be a monumental mistake.

Honor them with your achievements, just like you honor your parents. They are friends with knowledge. They are a voice of wisdom.

If you were looking to cheat time, this is a legal way, to learn from those who walked the path before and to avoid their mistakes. Most importantly, to be inspired and convince that it is possible.

The main role of a mentor is to erase the doubts that lay in your heart, even after jumping in the water and throwing away your armor.

I have the privilege to have many of those wise friends. I am grateful to them, all of them. They have their stories, their regrets and their medals. They also have their ghosts and their demons. We all do.

In the water, I will never forget the eyes of those looking down on me while frozen. Even though the water, the look wasn't pretty. So never again, will I have that look to anyone.

I attract mentors and friends, fans, and lovers because I stopped judging. We choose, and we bear the consequences. We don't need more layers than those.

Actually, who likes to be bullied? What is it to judge someone than to bully our views and values upon that person? There is nothing right about that. From the day I started ripping my armor and values, I try to stay as lightweight as possible.

"If I don't have much values (burdens), it becomes much easier not to impose those on anyone."
Dr. Bak Nguyen

This is how I became powerful and loved. This is how I attract people who choose to stay in my surroundings, my entourage. Friends, mentors, fans, lovers, those are my companions.

This is **MASTERMIND, 7 ways into the big league.** Welcome to **MILLION DOLLAR MINDSET**.

I am what I will and I'll be what I tried.
Dr. BAK NGUYEN

CHAPTER 6
"THE TRUE ACCEPTANCE"
by JONAS DIOP

I've tried a lot of things in my life. I tried to find my way like others. I went to university, but even with the years spent, I did not find my purpose in life nor what I really want to do. All my life, I was looking for stability, I wasn't asking for too much!

I had a rough childhood, raised by a strong woman with a strong personality. My siblings and I, had some challenges, some issues. I just wanted to say to my mom, to my family how much I love them, especially you, mama.

Reading Dr. Bak, it reminded me how those people who love us, tend to protect us by putting limitations and boundaries so we won't get hurt. Unfortunately, if you want to grow and become stronger, you will need to experiment to find your own path.

The sooner, the better since we will have more time, and by extension, more energy to learn, adapt, and thrive.

Sometimes you meet people who understand you beyond your word. With kindness and with wisdom,

Dr. Bak tells us to accept all the parts of ourselves, the light and the dark. We can capitalize on both of them.

Our pain, our frustration, our anger need to find a way to be expressed. I am doing as the doctor prescribed by writing this book and sharing with you.

"To be an alchemist,
transform the poison into nectar."
Jonas Diop

On the journey to discover ourselves, in our introspection, we will eventually take off some layers, some prejudices deeply implanted in your mind since childhood, some times from our parents, some times from our culture, our language etc…

Have you ever heard that money can't buy happiness? If it's the case, you probably have **ANTs: Automatic Negative Thoughts.** Dr. Bak taught us to call all the **bluffs of doubt** because doubt is just that, a big bluff. If you are afraid, the bluff will work, and you will be proving your doubts right!

Trust in your intuitions, and allow yourself to be free, to be **YOUR OWN SELF.**

We listen to others, often without much filtering, especially when it comes from a trusted source, from our loved ones. Too often, we don't even know where our fears come from.

What we hear splits us inside, what we feel, and what we believe became two different things. We have a broken connection within ourselves. How mess-up is that!

For a few years, we shallow the pill and accept to kneel down, bowing our head. But our body never forgets, and slowly the pain will be felt.

Our heart will cry in silence, our body will bleed and crack with pain and sadness, and we won't even know where this is coming from. This is where we go to our family doctor and start taking even more pills. This time, the pills are physical.

Do you now see clearly how the **bluff of doubt** works its way up the ladder to trick us? Dr. Bak calls gave it a name, **Conformity**. Bluff of doubt or Conformity, it all originated from the void inside, the void caused by our ignorance or denial of ourselves.

Facing our « identity », facing our cultural-psychological heritage, we have **3** choices.

1- To accept
2- To revolt against
3- To sort, taking what's good to us, and leaving the *extras*.

Dr. Bak is one of a few people capable of connecting with everyone. I saw the man in action many times over, I have to give him this unique ability.

When you meet in person with him, he is able to bring out the best of you, you just have to be open, listening, and aware. He has one of those vibes that lift you up and empower your heart.

Literally, you can feel your heart beating free. At his contact, you feel immediately re-energize, you feel better. I know I do!

I ask myself, where is this gift come from? How is he able to empower people, to empower me? So I asked him. Without hesitation, he told me his secret. He did so live and online when I first met him and invited him on my podcast.

By then, he was on the **YesMan's challenge:** for 18 months in a row, he was accepting all requests, for special cases, he must consult his life partner and **Mdex's** Vice-President Tranie Vo.

Being open, generated news opportunities, a new life, a breath of fresh air. His **YesMan's challenge** changed him at his core, pushing him to be stronger from his flexibility, to be more generous from his openness, to be more powerful, from his kindness.

His challenge also contributed to forge a strong friendship between us. For this, I am grateful. I saw, I was there. Now it is time to put actions to the words. Let's be open with people, let's welcome Life.

The main lesson the challenge taught Dr. Bak is to accept who you are. The only way to say **YES** to everything is not to judge. Since you are stopping the judgment, why keep judging yourself?

As a natural-born leader and someone that's master the art of **Momentum**, Dr. Bak is a force of Nature. Some people tried to slow him down, telling him what he needs to do. He has his own path, his own vision, he is laser-focus, don't try to curb a **Momentum**.

What is remarkable is that even if some tried to hurt him, I saw him keep his cool, his class and move on. He did not stop and fight back, settle the score, or seeking revenge. He is not stupid, he simply chooses to stay focus on the battle that really matters to him.

His generosity, his kindness, they didn't make a dent in any of them. If anything, he came out of it, even kinder and more generous.

But those who showed their true face and ugly heart, well, they missed out on a great man.

Like one of the great philosophers of all the time, Jiddu Krishnamurti said: you need to go inside of yourself to find the truth, to find the answers, to find peace.

Once you find yourself, you find love. You can be loyal because you know who you are and what you are made of. Only secured, can one give unconditional love to someone else.

You will open up and embrace that special someone in all their shades. You are creating a meaningful relationship based on interdependency. Together you will rise over the challenges.

To find yourself, you need to get rid of the prejudices, to free yourself of fears, to unlearn the faulty patterns of Conformity, to learn to trust and follow your intuition, to accept yourself. That's empowerment!

Dr. Bak and Jiddu Krishnamurti share the way to go into an introspection, to be the leader of your life, to re-learn who you are, to embrace yourself.

Are you ready to affirm your true essence? Are you ready to find your worth, to reach your infinite potential?

This is **MASTERMIND, 7 ways into the big league.** Welcome to **MILLION DOLLAR MINDSET**.

One decision can turn your life around, you just need to take it.

JONAS DIOP

CHAPTER 7

"DO YOU AGREE WITH THE THEORY OF WORK/LIFE BALANCE?"

by Dr. BAK NGUYEN

Honestly, I don't, and here is why. By now, you know that I am all about **Energy**. **Speed** is pure Energy, **Momentum** is Energy condense, so to me, this is the **core of Life**.

Of course, I believe that Life balanced itself, but Life is also much bigger than me. If I learned humility and my place in the Universe, this time, I should leverage on my advantage: I am nothing but a small part of the Universe, another part will balance myself.

In other words, I know that I am myself the respond to many inefficiencies and inertia. My **Speed** and **Momentum** are meant to balance that out. The balance is made at a much greater scale than without myself.

This is my **humility**; to recognize that I am within a much bigger ensemble and whole.

"I believe in the balance of the Universe. I am a little part of the Universe, little inside of a much greater scheme. So I am not balance itself."
Dr. Bak Nguyen

It sounds very poetic, don't you agree? Believe it on not, I slept on this answer for days before starting to write and elaborate on it. I stand by each and every word of my respond.

Does that means that I am an irresponsible bastard who just takes and does as he wishes? Absolutely not. I said I believe in the balance of the Universe, so everything I am given, I must render, amplified. Everything that I am, I must leverage, and everything that I see, I must make sense of.

I believe in free choice and its consequences. On that, my heart and mind are clear, everything that we do bears consequences. The consequences are often much broader than we thought since its ripple effect can be felt for miles and years around if you matter enough.

I am free, and I don't take anything lightly. I do not take myself seriously, but I never underestimate the impact of my work and my words. This is not presumptuous, if anything, it is kind and responsible.

I may have discarded most of the armor of Conformity, but I still bear the mark of its training and the titles. Being called Doctor is not a sign of prestige, but one of humility, the calling that people require your help.

This is also what has pushed me to dwell my questioning and my work as far, I must understand in order to help.

And since I am a respond to a broken system, a broken but functional system, what do I do? Do I destroy and build a new one to replace the old, or do I fix the broken, as imperfect as it might be?

Well, this is the kind of balance that I am bounded with: I was there to help, so to each action, its reaction, to each novelty, its price, to each solution, its collaterals.

This is my burden, I do not balance my decisions, nor my actions; the only way to have something new emerging was to give it all what I got. But before I do so, I had to weight its benefits in the balance, hoping that I have taken into account the collaterals. This is not about pride, it is about power and its liabilities.

Yeah, on that, for those seeking power, know that power can be intoxicating, but also that power comes with much, much liabilities. That's what I am trying to minimize.

"Influence is power without the liabilities."
Dr. Bak Nguyen

I am a lazy guy, always had and always be. So I look for the shorter path, the easier path, always. Since I am avoiding the path of power, Influence found me.

In the path of Influence, you still need to weight the pro and the cons, you still matter much, but the burden is somehow lesser.

"I do not balance, I leverage."
Dr. Bak Nguyen

To me, each question, as complex as they are, can be broken down into smaller and smaller pieces. I break them down until there is no hesitation between the good and the bad, and I solve that piece. Then, I move on to the next and the next.

Each night, before going to bed, I reunite all of the pieces assemble and see how they fit in the grand scheme. Some will fit, other, even perfect, will simply destroy the synergy and harmony that I am looking for. Those will have to go.

This is the secret of my creations and the process that keeps it relevant: to discard the inharmonic pieces, even if by themselves, they were perfect. The whole is the goal, not the individual pieces.

I discard those pieces, but no worries, I put much time and energy into them, I will keep them on for later until I can find good use to them.

Ideas are pretty much like humans. Some will disturb, some will empower, if we took the time to nurture and polish them, they could all shine, only we must found their rightful place first.

This is my equilibrium, to weight everything into the greater scheme. As for myself, I do not hold back from my work to have the time to enjoy life. I am enjoying my life since I am useful at what I do.

Even my family, those closest to me, are joining in my life work. Tranie, my best friend and wife, is also the co-founder of my companies. Without her input and participation, God knows how lost I would be.

William, my son, has joined my world, demanding to write books with his dad. We did, and together, we broke world records, one after the next. We are happy as a family because we empower one another.

On the personal side, I am still struggling to have everything aligned. My **willpower** and my vision are now forces to be dealt with, but my body has a hard time following. Is this age, is this fatigue, it is an inefficiency.

For years, I struggled with an overweight problem, even if I show up at the gym twice a week, even if I do my swimming laps, even if I know that I am pretty active.

I have to take it back to the **Energy formula**:

$$\text{ENERGY} \propto \frac{\substack{\text{WILL} \\ \text{DESIRE}}}{\text{VALUES}}$$

So to me, this boils down to two key factors: either I am still burdened with values that are foreign to my nature, or simpler, I must find more desires to empower.

Yes, I've been through my midlife crisis, and I know how the body, everyone's body, is reacting to the starving and the scarcity of the life regime that modern society is putting each of us through.

On the matter, I wrote a book, my 12th, **REBOOT, Growing from midlife crisis**. I invite each of you wanting to know more about yourself and your urge to dive into this one. You will find a normal mapping of your life's regime.

"Choices and consequences, it is as simple."
Dr. Bak Nguyen

Have you noticed that the equation is not an equal sign, but a proportional sign linking the Energy from the equation? It is so because even if two people are doing the exact same thing, with the same value, the same will and the same willpower, the Energy release will be different.

This is the main key that Conformity has eluded for so long, each of us is different, even if we are alike. No two equations will be the same, just like no two individuals can be one. Therefore, this is how I came up with the following:

"Perfection is a lie."
Dr. Bak Nguyen

Since no two equations will be the same, why bother trying to control everything to fit it to our pride? The recipe Conformity found is to cut out as much of the

Energy until it is small enough to be contained, to be foreseeable, to be controlled.

Again with that insecurity, control, and power. My friends, embrace **freedom** and **harmony**, **respect** and **love**. Doing so, who needs perfection, amputation, and control?

But **Balance** is a different aspect. It is not for control, but for harmony. So yes, I believe in balance, but in the greater scheme. On myself, I weight the pros/cons, and I give it my all, without holding anything back.

I raise my Energy for as much I need to fulfill my task in hand. I decrease and sort out my values until it is simple and light, in diapason with my true nature.

I found my will serving others and finding my rightful place in the Universe. My fun now is to find desires to empower! I do so with humility, with respect, and with gratitude.

> "I have and respect my history and my past, but I do not average my past with my future."
> Dr. Bak Nguyen

I believe there is a key difference between **Balancing** and **Averaging**. One is weighting the final result in the greater scheme, the other is to mix up the past in every future recipe.

Weren't we looking for a change, for improvement? How do you do that if you keep mixing it up with what you are trying to run from?

This is **MASTERMIND, 7 ways into the big league.** Welcome to **MILLION DOLLAR MINDSET**.

I am what I will, and I'll be what I tried.
Dr. BAK NGUYEN

CHAPTER 8
"THE HARMONY"
by JONAS DIOP

For over three decades, I was trapped by the illusion of Life balance. This theory gave me so much trouble, so many frustrations.

I thought something with me, how couldn't I understand and apply such a basic concept? I really tried, I did, but something seems broken. Until lately, I thought the broken was me!

At the beginning of my journey, as I was reading biographies of high achievers, I found them all crazy and bold, a little too extreme, so I went the opposite way. I embraced, no, I forced myself to shallow the common beliefs of life balance, to have an equal focus on everything.

I tried every method, I listen to every gurus, doing yoga, breathing exercises, meditation and some other stuff that I forgot the name… Name it, I tried them, all of them.

What came out of the entire experience was that I was in denial, plain and simple. To produce, I need to be in the zone to generate a lot of energy just to feel great. That's me, that's who I am, that's my pattern.

Honestly, I was shocked to find out that I love to feel the pain, to feel the exhaustion, to push my limits. I don't like the pain, but I don't care much about it. When there is pain, it serves as a reminder to keep moving. That's how I will generate **Energy**!

I fuel on adrenaline and movement. I am alive from my kinetic. I have always felt it, but now, I know it! I don't want balance, I want stability. Which isn't the same concept, but not at all. Please, allow me to clarify the difference between **Balance** and **Stability**.

Balance is when you are able to put the same amount of focus is all the areas of your life, and you are looking for equality. **Stability** is when you choose to put your focus on one particular aspect but in ways that don't affect your core and your life's flow.

Of course, things will change, but they are evolving, not starting a revolution. It's pretty much like learning something new, feeling it, and putting it on the back burner until you see the opportunity to leverage on it in the future.

But when it comes to production, to deliver on my talents, I put countless hours writing, reading, searching, planing, I do whatever it takes, but counting. Counting the hours is very contra-productive if you ask me.

On the field, to deliver and to produce, I am totally unbalanced, I focus all of my being and Energy on that task at hand, nothing else matters until I am done with my task.

As I received an SMS of encouragement from girlfriend to keep writing and to achieve this book, that's my stability, my driving force. I am stable because I know who I am and because I found love. I am unshakable.

I salute Dr. Bak for his humility. We are no Superman or Batman... maybe sometimes, but if you listen to the man for long enough, he will tell you that he has enough of his burdens, he doesn't need the one coming with a superhero status!

That's pure wisdom if you ask me. We can't do everything at the same time. We must plan, we must choose, we have to sort out and to prioritize to respect our current responsibilities. It's about evolving, not burning down the house to build a better one...with the same flaws within.

People are counting on us, for us, we make the right decisions and to face their consequences. That's called to be a human. If Dr. Bak doesn't believe in balance, that's the nuance he lives by, one that balances his drive and boldness with his kindness and generosity. If you really need to summarize it, it is **Respect** and **Awareness**.

Dr. Bak, as a mentor, is continuously reminding me to let go of everything that is not in harmony. If I don't, I will face a crisis sooner than I think. In the shoes of an entrepreneur, I will face burnout.

In our life, we have 8 main areas:

1- Spirituality   **5**- Professional

2- Material   **6**- Relationship

3- Finance   **7**- Family

4- Intellectual   **8**- Health

To be efficient and productive, we need to choose between 2 or 3 areas to focus on. Once we made our choices, you will dedicate most of your energy and concentration to evolve within those areas of your life.

And remember, there are no right or wrong answers here, just the one in harmony with your core and those of lesser importance.

"Choose freely, stay focus, and dedicate and you will grow. Choose your battles!"
Jonas Diop

As one Dr. Bak's protege, he wants me to elevate myself to reveal my true nature, to unleash my full potential. He says to leverage, one needs to focus on their advantages, on their talents and skills. But to really move forward, one also needs to be aware of his/her flaws. Not to double down on them, but to leverage eventually over them.

As an entrepreneur, I have plenty of people that can compete with me in different areas. I am aware, but I only care about how I can improve my services and my offers. To do so, I need to keep learning and discovering. What was great yesterday, is only good today and maybe outdated by tomorrow.

So to be dedicated and 100% commit to my expertise and offering, I need to focus on my task. That why all high achievers have a team to delegate to. As an entrepreneur, I do not do my own book-keeping, I hire an expert to do so. That's his job, mine is to grow my business.

In entrepreneurship, one of my main inspirations is Gary Vaynerchuck, the social media guru. I really like his work ethic. He is working like a machine for 5 days a week. He is intense, always moving, he is a man of action.

He has dreams, and he strives for them: He wants to buy the New York Jets, yes, the Baseball Team. **Momentum** is around him all time long, he is looking at opportunities in different ways. Thanks to his speed, he is reducing the risk factor; with his certainty, he is decreasing the friction.

He was building one of his first business called **Library Wine Tv**, on YouTube, when no one else was active in the field. Just look for his video « overnight success » that is such an inspiration.

If you are obsessed with balancing in your life, in all areas, your action process will slow down, and your impact will diminish. That's a certainty.

Well, I have a secret for you. Your best decision is often the first one. Like in Mel Robbins' book, **The Five Seconds Rule**, just count 5,4,3,2,1 to make a decision, and take your action.

Gary Vaynerchuck and Dr.Bak, both have an incredible work ethic. When they are in their working process, they are like war machines, but they also take time for their families. They know about the 8 areas and have chosen their battles wisely.

They believe in leveraging time to impact, to inspire, to exceed their own expectations. They are looking for **stability**, not **balance**. They are looking for **harmony**.

Choose 3 areas of your life that you want to improve. Write down 10 actions for each area. Write down simple steps that are within your reach. Take the top 3, and let's go!

This is **MASTERMIND, 7 ways into the big league.** Welcome to **MILLION DOLLAR MINDSET**.

One decision can turn your life around, you just need to take it.

JONAS DIOP

CHAPTER 9

"HOW DO YOU RECOGNIZE OPPORTUNITIES?"

by Dr. BAK NGUYEN

Finally, after the why and the how, here comes the what? If we stuck with the **Energy formula**, this one is the easy one. The how is the equation, the why in my case was the fear of God (I'll tell you the story later) and the presence of William.

Since I worked on myself and get rid of my **armor of Conformity**, I discover my powers, **Speed,** and **Momentum**. In other words, I have released much energy and now need purposes to put that energy to good use.

The only variable left in the equation is **DESIRE**. This should be easy, no? Actually, it is not as simple as it might first seem. My **Quest of Identity** was about myself, but my legend can't be one about myself. Otherwise, it will have no power and no impact.

> "To enhance your power, find your worth."
> Dr. Bak Nguyen

And my worth is found when I am at the service of others. This is how it balances out. All of the power I found, all of the potential I have at my disposal, all of those can only make sense with a purpose bigger than myself.

Sure, I sometimes serve my own desires, but those usually last for not more than a few hours and are always harder to see through. But every time that I am helping someone else to clarify and materialize their desire, my power grew exponentially.

This is how I identify the opportunities, looking for desires. I am to say that I did more than that, I push further. Most of the time, people have desires that are buried with doubts and hesitation.

But when their will of change is big enough, it is a wonderful journey to travel to help them realize their hopes and open up to the magic of Life, of Abundance.

If I have to feed on something, this is it. I love the feeling of accomplishment and the joy of satisfaction. Since I will never reach satisfaction myself, I am very grateful to share these moments with those I help.

Before, when I had a smaller mind, I was doing the same, but expecting gratefulness and recognition in return. Well, Life taught me to expect nothing from anyone but myself. I had to train myself even harder to stay open and generous and to remove the expectation part. It is called not to get attached.

It doesn't mean not to care, it only mean not to expect anything from anyone but yourself. Somehow, that was a remanent of the victim's mentality. I am no victim, I make it happen.

To free myself from the expectation of others and from my own expectations of the others, I threw away one of the main plates of armor covering my chest. Since that day, I can't tell you how free and powerful I am.

What Conformity gave me, telling me it will protect my heart, was actually torturing it! The worst part is that I believe that lie for so long.

"The final cure to Conformity is to get rid
of all expectations."
Dr. Bak Nguyen

No one can predict what will happen. No one should. Life is supposed to be fun, where is the fun when you know where, when, and how it will happen? It will cost much to arrive as such a prediction, and you are mainly killing the **buzz of Life**!

You can't be happy within expectations, even if you achieve all of them! Trust me, I walked the path for decades, only to find out that it will never be enough and that no one, I said, no one had any pleasure out of it. **Expectations** and **Pretentions** are very close siblings.

And yet, we were discussing the opportunity! You want to create opportunity out of thin air, look for desire. Not yours, yours will be the weakest one. Look for the desires of others to empower.

This is how I build my success in the past 20 years. I started with the desire of a patient desperate to be in a dental chair.

Then, I empower the desire of those lacking confidence and wanting to look and feel better. I became a cosmetic surgeon in dentistry.

After years of changing the world a smile at a time, I then embrace the feeling better more than the looking better. This is how I changed the model of a complete industry, the dental industry.

I didn't stop there, there were still so many desires and needs I watched on. I keep pushing embracing the feeling of a better mentality, and I wrote about it. One book after the next, always pushing the boundaries a little further at each next book.

I did that on paper and also on the web, through posts, quotes, videos, and lives. Today, I have a hard time getting out of my office without meeting with smiles of strangers looking to shake my hand.

I always feel observed, and the minute that my eyes cross those looking at me, a smile appears, and people are approaching looking to tell me how I inspire them.

This is all very new to me. But this is what I now attract, recognition, and gratitude. Recognition I don't know, but gratitude is the value that stuck with me, even after the painful purge and the visceral ripping.

"You attract what you are."
Dr. Bak Nguyen

It can't be any straight forward. Think it, say be, hear it, and be it. Sooner than you think, you will be attracting what you thought, what you said, what you heard, and what you are.

Today, more than ever, it is easier and easier for me to identify the needs and the desire of people. Today, people are knocking at my door and tell me about their desires and their needs.

With evolution, some people are now knocking at my door only to thank me for having empowered them to look for their own solution.

Isn't it beautiful? If you were wondering how my power grew, this is a great example to illustrate it. Before, people came to me, because they trusted me and because they have hope.

They came with their problems and then, their hopes. I have to work my magic to see their smiles. Each time, I see a soul opening up and embracing Life with new eyes of Hope. If I was in power, this was my moment of glory.

Today, people are coming to me, thanking me for inspiring them. Some people already said how much I had changed their life… I didn't even know them. But this is the new magic, the power without liability: I now influence and inspire people!

From my writings, from my posts, from my quotes, I touched people's life being myself and walking my own path. I achieved such because I am genuine and committed. I shared, and I am available to listen, not for opinions, not for feedbacks, but for testimonials.

"Opinions are cheap, feedbacks are opinions.
Testimonials, on the other hand, require commitment.
And commitment, I can relate to."
Dr. Bak Nguyen

Are you still looking for how I identify and create opportunities? I attract them to me. I inspire people to open up and to share with me. They share their dreams, their hopes, their desires, their problems. I listen, I encourage, I share my views, I empower.

This is my new formula to create opportunities. Since people have endless desires and the world is full of people, I will not run out of options any time soon.

Find yourself, find your worth and serve. This is the path to power. With time, your powers will have a ripple effect. Be aware of the echo of your actions and you will discover a new form of power, one without liability: **Influence**.

"Influence is power without liability."
Dr. Bak Nguyen

And once you have achieved **Influence**, you won't have to go look for opportunities, tell with come knocking at your doors. You'll then have to listen and sort.

I became as such because I unbalanced myself and put everything, risk everything to push forward. I used myself, my whole being, as a leverage to break free.

Now my entire being is a tool for change, one people can leverage on for their own liberation.

I see the desires, I respect their needs. I help them to find confidence in themselves and encourage them to jump in the water and to start their journey.

This is my opportunity, this is who I am. I am Dr. Bak. Open your heart to help, open your mind to learn and you will be creating opportunities as you breathe.

This is **MASTERMIND, 7 ways into the big league.** Welcome to **MILLION DOLLAR MINDSET**.

I am what I will and I'll be what I tried.

Dr. BAK NGUYEN

CHAPTER 10

"ALWAYS THE HEART FIRST"

by JONAS DIOP

I come from the suburb of Paris, France. Where I am from, we don't have opportunities like others. We do not have a silver spoon in our mouth. Just like many of you, we face multiples obstacles because of our cultural background, our social state, our skin colors.

"I don't call that injustice, I call that life."
Jonas Diop

We were not created equal, I made my peace with that. What I do though, is to make the most of what I've received, of who I am.

I enjoy my situation as a black man in this society. To me, it's a blessing, one I can easily create a legacy from. I have nothing to prove to anyone but to myself.

I have nothing to protect, to slow me down. So I can leverage all of my being to build. I am an underdog.

My entrepreneurial career started at the age of 4. At school, I went to the playground and saw the other children with snacks: Kinder surprise, Prince, BN, etc.. I did not have one.

Children play games, I was skillful. I won beads, playing cards and traded them for snacks. I hustled, I created opportunities, I was the middle man, and I was 4. If someone needed something, I was the child to go to. I always found a way to realize his wish.

Being at the service of others, Dr. Bak never forgot the fundamental principle to genuinely connect first. We need to focus on other people's desires first to be able to achieve our own. To be open, to listen carefully, and to help without looking for gratefulness or recognition.

I heard a long time ago that if we share something material, we are dividing it. But when we share something immaterial, we are multiplying it! Were we looking for **Abundance**?

There is never a right moment to be kind, to help people, to listen, to care because, at the end of the day, we are trading objects or services, but we are not doing **B2B** (Business o Business), or **B2C** (Business to Customer), we are connecting **H2H**, humans to humans.

This is the only way we can help each other to be better, to feel better.

Dr. Bak mission's as a surgeon is to empower people, to give them values for them to open up. Once they do that, they will discover new angles, another world, a world full of opportunities.

People share with you, connect with you, give you values and worth. That's the **law of the mirror**, it is mirroring what you gave them.

A great example and role model on the matter is the founder of Zappos: Tony Hsieh. In his book **Delivering Happiness**, he shares his business philosophy to make employees and customers happy.

He focused on building a great customer experience with the **WOW EFFECT**. One of the employees' rules was never to be the one hanging up the phone, if a customer had a bad day and needed to talk, they would listen, almost as a friend, until the client felt better.

Customers were amazed and started spreading their Zappos' experience all around. **Mdex & Co** shares the same philosophy.

In July 2009, Zappos, e-commerce based company selling shoes, was sold to Amazon for nearly one billion dollars. And they had no way to put a real value on all the happiness the company spread around throughout the years, on both the customer and employees. Because spreading happiness brings in even more happiness!

Tony Hsieh and Dr. Bak know at their core, the importance of taking care of people, the importance of creating an atmosphere of happiness, one of empowerment to give values all the parties. But if you ask them, that was natural, it was about being a **decent human**.

The person in front of you is really important because if you listen carefully, that you are genuinely trying to help, he/she will feel it and will open up to you. He/she will share with you their problems and resources, and you share your energy and kindness. They will be pretty happy since they just found in you an ally.

You were looking for ways to create resources, be kind, be helpful. That's how you will find your worth. Opportunities start with you being yourself, you in harmony with your surroundings. Once you are in **harmony**, you are an opportunity, an opportunity for people to feel better, to realize their dreams and ambitions.

You are rocking this book, you are rocking the path to the **big league**, you are growing faster than you know.

This is **MASTERMIND, 7 ways into the big league.** Welcome to **MILLION DOLLAR MINDSET**.

One decision can turn your life around, you just need to take it.

JONAS DIOP

CHAPTER 11
"HOW DO YOU CREATE LEVERAGE?"
by Dr. BAK NGUYEN

This is an excellent question, one that will require more thinking before I can give you a straight answer. Let's start by defining what leverage is.

Leverage is a way to use a tool or a stratagem to achieve the cantilever effect, to produce more energy than what I've put in. In a Universe where the main law is nothing is ever created nor destroyed, where everything will balance, leveraging is cheating, a legal way to cheat!

That's why I like it so much, it is cheating using our creativity and curiosity. The result of leverage, in the long run, is the formation of a system. Look around you, we built a life upon systems, systems upon systems.

So the first I will advise anyone to take is to take a system familiar to you, choose the one you love and know the most, and take it apart to see how it works. Reversed engineer the system to understand its composition and how they fit together.

You are an engineer, take a clock apart and study it. You are a gamer, take a computer apart and study it.

You are an actor, take your favorite script apart and study each component.

You are a doctor, well go sit in a classroom, a children's classroom and listen to how it started building up. Then, look at yourself and revisit your own story. From that journey, you might figure out more than you've bargained for…

To take apart is not to destroy. To take apart means to remove the layers one by one and to understand their function and synergy with the other component. Now that you have undone the system, you still have all the pieces; you must put it back together, so it works again.

This is the tricky part, what seems logical and simple before is suddenly not the same as you have the responsibility to fit the pieces back together. You will soon learn to appreciate the effort and the geniuses of those who made the system before you start criticizing again.

That's good, you are learning **Humility** and **Gratitude**. Those weren't the main goal of the process, but there are surely great benefits, especially when they are coming as side effects.

It might take more than one try before you could put back all the pieces together. That's okay, it was nothing but a simulation. Then, once you put all the pieces together, take them apart once more, and rebuild the system again. Do so to knock the psychological wall before it rises.

The goal was not to be impressed nor proud of understanding a system but to make a habit of deconstructing to learn and to build it back up as soon and as quickly as possible.

Then, move on to another system and another. Soon enough, you will have learned from the greater among us, the builders, and those who still bear the pillar of our civilization on the back.

Earlier, you ask me what kind of company I look forward to, well, this is the kind of inspiriting company that I recommend. So you've learned with reversed engineering in the company of the great minds throughout time and space.

You've learned thought **humility, respect,** and **gratitude** the worth of those people and how they are serving you, even without you noticing. This is what you should aim for, that kind of recognition is more subtle, but will leave its mark forever in the next generations of builders.

This is what you've become, part of the next generations of builders. You studied the systems, and you know how they were put together. You didn't learn their recipe, you learned the logic and the ingeniosity to inspire yourself from.

Well, this is the path of a builder. Is it okay if I show you how to jazz up the game a little bit? Well, I have much fun taking those systems apart and combining them back together to form a new system.

I use the spare parts of one system to replace the core of another. Since I know how the pieces interact together, I can play with them and rearrange them as I please.

And I learn from the result. If the outcome is not what I was hoping for, I deconstruct it was reassembled another system. In between, I sometimes force myself to rebuild a known system, just to reconnect with that great mind and his/her way of thinking.

I leverage is that I understand the systems of society and of Conformity. I also understand engineering and reverse engineering. So I have those to play with, in my toolbox, to construct and deconstruct social systems.

Each time I learn a new system, I learn a new blueprint, but also, sometimes, I end up with new and original spare parts. If you want a simple example of this, just think of each system as a LEGO CONSTRUCTION SET.

Buy one and build up the set according to the instructions. Then, take it apart and use the pieces for something of your own creation. So you bought a LEGO CAR SET. Then, you bought a LEGO TRAIN with the motor and the rails. Can you combine the two of them together?

And then, you bought the MIND STORM LEGO SET with the programmable sensors, can you make use of those? Can you have much fun finding out what to do with the possible combinations? This is leveraging.

"Leveraging is to take the past as spare parts and to combine it as an element of the future system."
Dr. Bak Nguyen

I don't think that I could summarize it any clearer nor with more precision. Leveraging is to package the past in ways to use it as a building block for the future.

This is how I leverage my life. My past good or bad, I package what can be useful, I edited and aligned the pieces of the narrative to serve a purpose, and I repackage it for future use.

When I said that you must channel your emotions, good and bad, this is how I channel them, packaging them into building blocks to build upon or fuel to feed my **Momentum** with.

This is leveraging taken apart so you can understand the process and the logic. It is leveraging 101. But what about its use in everyday real life?

NARRATIVE is one of my leverage of choice. A narrative is a story you are telling people. The narrative will allow you to position yourself in the past and to tell the story of how and why you became who you are today. It will also give a chance for people to relate to you, in other words, to love you!

Well, the great stories of my past always started with a point in time that I was lost and desperate to find hope. Each of my past **"bad" emotions** are great starting points for a new narrative.

> "Find leverage out of your liability
> to always move forward."
> **Dr. Bak Nguyen**

You read that quote from me more than once if you are following my journey. This is a great way to illustrate what I meant by leveraging your liability, your past. Hey, you paid the price already, why not make the most out of it?

Surprisingly, your **NARRATIVE** will do more than helping connect with people. Your **NARRATIVE** will begin by relating you with people. Then, as they are in your shoes, they will relate with you, and soon enough, they will identify with you. Not just your thinking, but your emotions too.

They will feel as they know you and that you are already a part of their life. You achieved that by sharing openly, genuinely, and with honesty. Now you have people looking to touch and to be inspired by you. In another time and epoch, we would have called them followers and disciples...

But you do not want that. They have their own personal journey to attend, and you still have yours. Let just say that you have influence and an army of fans!

Isn't this powerful? This is the power of leveraging a **NARRATIVE**.

*"People love stories, they can feel them
so they might believe them."*
Dr. Bak Nguyen

Still looking for more? How about **leveraging Time**? I know you love this one! How can you leverage Time? By seeing it as abundant and none linear.

If you wake up in the morning a have an organized schedule for every 15 minutes, you will be very productive. You will have leveraged your organizational skills to gain efficiency, but you won't have leverage on Time itself.

To leverage on Time means to bend Time, to create more Time. Is this even possible? This has the merit of its own chapter, not just an example in one. But I've started already. Well, here it is:

If you want to cheat Time, you have to outpace it. Either you are faster than the clock, either you are slower, either way, you will obtain the same effect.

I told you that my powers are **Speed** and **Momentum**. Well, I cheat Time by outpacing it. Here's a simple application in the dental chair.

More than fast, I am also very empathic as a dentist. I know that most, if not all, of my patients hate to be in the dental chair. I share their feeling and am not shy to express it bluntly and candidly. So we connect.

I then reassure them by explaining the procedure with calm and confidence, taking my time to answer the questions and the fears. Often, the tone of my voice is enough to reassure them.

With a palm on their shoulders, I will tell them that it is okay and I will wake them up when I am done.

I say this joke as I put the chair in the operating position. They still look into my eyes for comfort. Their stress, I absorb, this is the only way that I've found. And then, I operate, knowing what to go for, I go in, score, and get out as quickly as possible, with calm and ease.

Between their fears and expectation and my speed, I often raise the chair, saying that it is almost done. Then, they look at me wondering what else needed to be addressed… well, it went so fast that I've missed my shoot to hurt you… and we all laugh.

Most of the time, not more than two or three songs have passed on the speakers. In other words, the whole operation took 10 to 15 minutes on average. If you ask them, my team or even myself, it felt like it was much longer.

Looking at what I did in the mouth, I look like it was much longer too, but the clock confirms to us that it was just that, 10 to 15 minutes.

It felt like going into space and escaping the law of gravity of a little while. It is not just about the efficiency, but how we all felt out of that operation.

The patient has his/her hope replenished, crushed most of his/her fear; my team and I experienced a wonderful feeling of achievement, surfing on both Time and Fear.

I did so because I wasn't in any rush to deliver. I was calm and had all the time in the world to operate. That, my patient felt too.

I achieved so thanks to my training and the training of my teammates who are listening and respond to the operation as I needed them to react. We often don't even have to talk to communicate, my team knows what is coming next and what will be needed.

By the end of each of my operating days, we might be exhausted, but every time, we felt happy, satisfied to have served with the best of our abilities, and living an "out of body experience".

Well, what happened in the dental chair on a daily basis, slowly morphed into my daily writing. I can write and won't stop until I am done. What feels like hours and hours of reflection usually was 60 to 90 minutes in real life.

This time, I am not sharing in real-time with a team or a patient, but with all of you, people that are strangers to me, people that are not even born at the time of this writing. I feel you all, I connect with you all, and together we shared the vibe of the moment, elevating our spirit.

The feeling is addictive. I can easily find my way back to it, but I need to be producing. The artists call it inspiration, the athletes, to be in the zone, the extreme athletes, to be one with the flow.

No matter how you name it, give yourself 100% for the task. Be present and fully aware for the moment, and you will create that pocket defining time and space, one during which you will have achieved and felt more than the linear arrhythmic timeline you woke up with.

This is leveraging **Time**. I am not sure that it can be taught, but it can surely be experienced by anyone. An easy way in is to play music. You don't have to be good at the instrument you are playing; you just have to enjoy it to the point that Time has no more effect on you.

This is how some musicians will be playing for hours before noticing it. They aren't tired, they were having fun. Gamers will also recognize the phenomena when they are so immersed in a game that they can go for hours without eating or drinking…

Find your own way in. The key to leverage Time is to feel and to enjoy. To know that Abundance is within reach and that you have the right to such abundance.

"Abundance of Time, of opportunities,
of energy, of resources."
Dr. Bak Nguyen

This could have sounded like BS, but I have shown you how to create each of the elements mentioned, have I not? **Opportunities**, **Energy**, resources, even **Time**!

This is **MASTERMIND, 7 ways into the big league.** Welcome to **MILLION DOLLAR MINDSET**.

I am what I will, and I'll be what I tried.
Dr. BAK NGUYEN

CHAPTER 12

"REWRITING THE RULES"

by JONAS DIOP

As a success strategist, my job is to teach people to leverage their resources. My clients' requests are to be faster, quicker, stronger, smarter. I use to answer that request with the implementation of a routine, a system to generate results. It is as simple as that.

A system is an ensemble of procedures and tools to achieve a goal. The more you learn and practice a system, the sooner you'll be mastering it. Then, as you are in total control, you can tweak the system to custom it to your needs, you will correct the system and maybe, even optimize it.

One the best book that I ever read is **Rich Dad, Poor Dad,** by Robert Kiyosaki. Robert explains to us the fundamental differences between his two dads, one being his own dad and the other being the dad of his best friend.

Both his dad wanted the best for him. But one was a scholar and a high ranking officer in the government, the other was a man without a high school degree, but as he died, he was the wealthiest man of the state of Hawaii.

His rich dad, like Dr. Bak, taught him to reverse engineer a system and to build his own. The other dad taught him to stand in line and to follow the trend. One lived in abundance for the second half of his life. The other, struggled financially for most of his life. Guess who is who.

You might have the same tools as anyone else, 24 hours a day, the same financial system, but if you don't break down the operations and procedures, you won't be playing the same game, since the rules are not the same to everyone. Not because it was unfair, simply because you stopped at what people are telling you.

It is only when you immerse yourself completely in a system that you can understand its mechanism and logic that you can leverage on it. In finance, it is called edging. In sport, it is called bending the limits. In business, it is called entrepreneurship, smart entrepreneurship!

Dr. Bak and I, had a discussion about how to gain **Momentum**, how to enter the **state of Flow**. You'll need to be dedicated and completely immerse in that specific world, some times, with your own soundtrack. This is one of Dr. Bak's secret, he has a playlist of soundtracks that put him in the **ZONE** within the minutes he pressed play.

I am following his lead. This is how I am writing and delivering on my promise to have a book published within a week. I started reading Dr. Bak's answers, I put down my annotations in my notebook.

Some ideas emerge, I put them together, draw a concept to make sense of them. I play with the subjects, making one interact with the other to experiment, to rewire the logic.

You should try it, it is a wonderful and pleasing experience, to play with the big ideas and to rearrange them in different orders and configurations.

I now understand how Dr. Bak uses his creativity, he doesn't always create new dots, new rules, nor a new system. Often, he rearranges the dots differently and making new associations. From there, he can explore a new line of logic.

I am used to train from seminars, books, and formation. Writing is an original concept to evolve and push the boundaries of self-improvement. Dr. Bak did that for the last 2 years, and he has achieved so much! World record achievements!

I am following his footsteps and jumping headfirst, co-writing with him this book. And then, I learn to observe the world and to de-construct it. Once you've tried, you won't ever see the world the same. Until then, I was building a brick at a time, from the ground up.

Now, reverse engineering the system, I apply the concept to my inspirational speeches to adapt to my writing. I am learning more about myself. Not my boundaries and my potential, but about my voice and my preference.

Dr. Bak sat down with me as I was stuck, looking for both time and inspiration. He told me that my strength is within my voice when I speak. He told me to speak and listen to my own words, then to write down those words I just heard.

Well, I did just that. Right now, I am not writing, I am speaking. And guess what, I am about to finish my 5th chapter today, the last day of the challenge!

I am in the zone, I leverage my skill to talk, I leverage my time. I leverage the teaching of my mentor. I am in beast mode.

"Advice can change your life for the best."
Jonas Diop

Just remember to take the time to plan, to see the horizon first. if you work smarter, not just harder, if you allow yourself to seek help, and as you do so, you will multiply your productivity by a **factor 10X**. **10X** your life, **10X** your impact.

To illustrate the concept, let's look at Russell Brunson, an entrepreneur, a genius in sales funnels. He is the founder of **Clickfunnel**. Within the last 3 years, his company goes from zero to 100 million dollars in revenue. 100 million, do I have your attention now?

He broke down all the online closing sales systems and readapted them for maximum optimization. Companies and CEOs are throwing millions and millions of dollars for their ability to leverage their business to the next level.

Like him, you just need to pay attention to the process, to the tools and the rules. You can understand the system, but you'll need to understand the underline logic first before you can reproduce it and leverage it to reach the infinite.

Russell Brunson and Dr.Bak are paying attention to built systems. They are paying attention to the universe around them, to perceive all the sublimities that can improve and empower their **Momentum** and bend **Time** itself.

Remember what's Dr.Bak said:

"you can cheat, legally, by learning
about shortcuts and leveraging."
Dr. Bak Nguyen

This is your time now! Are you ready to fly and to overachieve?

This is **MASTERMIND, 7 ways into the big league.** Welcome to **MILLION DOLLAR MINDSET**.

One decision can turn your life around, you just need to take it.

JONAS DIOP

CHAPTER 13

"WHAT DO I WANT TO LEAVE AS LEGACY?"

by Dr. BAK NGUYEN

Legacy, I am not that old! I am both flatter and a little lost that the question of **Legacy** is brought on the table. Well, I guess I should stick with the flattering.

I am all about the future. The past, unless I can leverage, it has no or little value to me. As you read before, I do package the past into building block I can build on, this is called leveraging in my vocabulary.

"Gratitude is the only past with a future."
Dr. Bak Nguyen

It is what it is. I am grateful to the past, I will honor what I have received by delivering as much as I can. I will do so to honor my parents and the people who believed in me, but I am doing so out of the **Fear of God**.

At the beginning of the book, I mentioned the **Fear of God**. So let's cover that subject. I was raised as a Catholic Christian attending church each Sunday for almost 20 years. The Bible, I knew much of it.

And then, I started reading more and more, other books than the Bible. I started talking and exchanging with people from all horizons. As I traveled throughout the years, visiting the ruins and History, I couldn't make sense of my fading Faith. Visiting Rome and the Vatican gave my Faith its fatal blow.

Even though I am not a stronger believer of the church anymore, I am a man of God, one that believes that there is a supreme intelligence way above our comprehension.

This is also why I do not believe in intermediaries between God and man since all of the intermediaries will only taint God with their limited Humanity.

But in the process of liberating myself, my past in so entangled with Religion that it will be hypocrisy to think that I am not influenced by its thinking.

So, from my roots, there is one particular story of the Bible that kept my flame going: the story of the Master and his three servants.

In short, the Master has to go away for a year. I call in his three servants. To the first one, he gave three talents, the second two and the last one, one. Talent, in ancient Rome, is money. Today I am amused by the twist of words.

A year later, the Master comes back and calls on his servants. The first one presents the three talents he received and three more. The Master was happy.

The second presents the two talents that he received and two more. The Master was happy. Then, the last servant went out running in the field to dig up the talent that he received.

I found it and come back to his Master, presenting a talent covered with dirt saying that he received that talent, but fear of losing it, he dug a hole to keep it safe.

The Master was furious, he fired the lazy servant and gave his talent to his first servant, the one with six already. The moral of the story is that we received from God gifts proportional to our skills. But as we received, we must deliver.

Well, that story I get and know pretty well. The twist happened when I dreamt of being in from of God. "God, you gave me three talents, here they are and here three more." Then, God will stand up from his throne and looking down on me, saying: "What are you talking about? I gave you ten!"

And I woke up sweating for an hour after the fact. It killed my night and the following days. I will be out of time, there is nothing to say to that! Since I have based most of my life preparing for that moment in front of God.

I don't know how many talents I've received, but I am delivering on all that I know. You wanted to know how I keep myself motivated? With the **Fear of God**. Here's the funny twist thought.

As I am delivering, I often found a new talent. "Oh, I did not know that I could do that, and that…" I am amazed and happy for literally 5 minutes, 6 to the max. And then, I realize that I will have to deliver on that one too!

So this is why I am overachieving and overdelivering, all the time. I do not know when I will have to face God, but I will have no regret, I will have delivered on everything that I know of.

This **Fear of God** helped me developed my **Speed** and, in time, my **Momentum**. In finance, we all know that there are only to emotions governing the traders, **Greed,** and **Fear**. And we also know that Fear is much much stronger than Greed since it is deeply rooted in our physiology.

Well, my nightmare free me from most of my fears, since the only one I have is not from this world! Put differently, I basically live my life fearlessly!

How good of a twist is that one? Of course, just like you, I have my doubts and my fears. But compare to the Fear of God, I do not freeze nor procrastinate, I find a way to deliver or I die trying!

This is all that a man can bear on his shoulders, to make it happen or to die trying. I am a man, one that received much from God. The more I received, the more fearful I grow of the final judgment. The more fearful I grew, the more powerful I become since I render and deliver more and more on the field.

Is this a cool story, I will let God and each one of you to decide. Personally, I made my peace with my **Destiny**, and I will keep running. This is my mindset, but over time, it has become my nature and my core.

So what Legacy am I looking to leave behind me? I do not care for as long as it pleases God. I like to think that the day I die, I will still be too busy planning for the years to come.

Something in me tells me that even when I'll be gone, people will still be working on my plans for a long, long time.

"Everything out of my power, I simply do not care!"
Dr. Bak Nguyen

It is one thing to have an overachieving mindset, it is other to live with one day in and day out. The only way to cope with the pressure, the failures, the unsatisfaction, and the happiness is not to get attached to anything nor anyone. Easier said than done.

I also grew wise enough to remove judgment and expectations from my table. I move forward as light as possible since what is ahead will require all of my being, experience, and knowledge even to stand a chance. That I know, I'm the one who provoked it!

You wonder how to make things happen, to materialize an idea?

I think it, I see it, I say it.
I then feel it and act on it.
I do as such three times over
And any ideals will turn
Into steel.

Give it a try, and you will be surprised by the power of your mind. Couple this with the **Energy formula** and you have all you need to move forward, as long as you've solved your Quest of Identity first.

That was the first step, one that no one can skip.

This is my experience and testimony at 42. I am sure, at least, I hope that by 50, I will have learned something new, some variances and nuances. But I can tell you that I live by the ideas and words within this book.

I can also tell you that this might not be the only way, but it is a good way to find your potential and to reach the power you hold inside.

Stay open and flexible, be kind and generous to serve the desires of others, it is always easier than to serve your own. Why? Because, the others will give you their resources to do so.

Helping them to reach their desires, you will be better and better at it, until you become good, delivering on desires. Can you see your worth and Influence by then?

Know your power, but if you ask me, do not seek power, it is not worth it.

"Happiness is worth it.
Power has too many liabilities attached to it."
Dr. Bak Nguyen

But you will still have to deliver. Well, try **Influence**, power without liability! Stay light and simple; it was painful enough the first time that we had to rip off the shiny armor of **Conformity**, are you ready to forge a new one?

Look for happiness and look for energy. Doing so, you'll know who will help you, and you will sense those you do not want around you.

Just close your eyes and follow your heart, you know more than you see.

If anything, this is my Legacy. You are my Legacy. As you find your happiness, purpose, and power, you are part of my Legacy, a legacy made of both the past and the future, one that God might like.

I am Dr. Bak, and this is only the beginning of my legend.

This is **MASTERMIND, 7 ways into the big league.** Welcome to **MILLION DOLLAR MINDSET**.

I am what I will, and I'll be what I tried.

Dr. BAK NGUYEN

CHAPTER 14
"A KISS FROM A ROSE"
by JONAS DIOP

I watch the Olympics, I watch boxing championship, I am a huge fan of the NBA, all of theses athletes wanting nothing more than to leave their mark, and be part of history. Some of them, for the glory, others to see their achievement.

I see public figures doing wonderful acts in silence, discreet in the shadow since they just want to make a better world as they are **giving back**. As I started my journey on the road to success, I was obsessed with being the best, to be a legend.

But something felt off. I wasn't aligned with my heart. I was under the influence of my pride. My mom slapped me behind the head and set my march straight, giving me those core values that today, I made part of my core identity, I did that willingly and from my freewill.

One of those primal values is to be available and ready **to help anyone**. No matter your status, your education, the colour of your skill, nothing distinguishes somebody in need. I will help you, that what Mama taught me. She raised me well.

How can I do that? How can I help anyone? I have my fears, my limitations, my needs too! The remedy was in an exercise new to me, at that time: **EMPATHY**.

EMPATHY is the ability to feel and understand what someone else is feeling. It is a special kind of ability, master it well, and it will become a superpower!

As I flew across the ocean to land in a new continent, a whole new world, I had hoped, but I was also lost and alone. At a certain point, I was completely lost, scared and needed help.

Then, I remembered what my Mama taught me, my purpose in Life: to help others. I also remembered that back in the schoolyard, I didn't have any snacks, but I also never went hungry.

I leverage my hunger to find the skill that would be valued to those around me. Soon enough, I was among the popular kid, someone to go to. That's my cause, my worth: to empower and help others.

I spent the next several years educating myself with philosophy and self-improvement technics. I really wanted to help people, to empower them, to free them from their fears, to be part of their success story, liberating them from expectations, and the heavyweight of doubt on their shoulders. So I became a performance and business coach.

On my journey helping others, I met all kinds of people, rich and poor, winners and losers, drivers and liars. Some have more potential than others. But at their core, they all share a hope, to be better!

On that, I totally agree with Dr. Bak. You have to take your past as the fuel to feed your resilience and determination to move forward, seeking a better place for yourself and those you love.

We are born winners, we have plenty of talents inside each of us. We just need to recognize our value and let them express themselves, freely, believing, and acting as if there were no limits.

"Fear is a call to live. Fear produces energy,
but Greed produces a plan."
Jonas Diop

FEAR and **GREED** are neither good or bad if you know how to use it properly. I am leveraging on them as we speak, using them to finish this last chapter. I am greedy to have my first book in English out, published, and available to the world to read.

At the same time, I am fearful not to respect my engagement with people that put their trust and their hope in me. I know that I will not let them down, but until it is done, I am not sure that I can deliver to meet their expectations and within the delays.

Dr.Bak and I, we are not trying to be famous, we are simply doing our part to inspire people to live up to their full potential, to be happy.

On both our journey, we have come to terms with our mission in Life: we have the power; therefore, the responsibility to empower the other. So we do it. It is as simple as that, we just want to be happy too. Those expectations we face are nothing but our own expectation toward ourselves.

I am really not surprised by Dr. Bak's answer in his last chapter. He is on the **path of the visionary**. If you are familiar with the **Pyramid of Maslow**, the last stage is to **give back**.

This book is a way to give back. We are open to receive your comments and appreciations, to share the energy, to learn and exchange with and from you.

We are improving ourselves on a daily basis to be better people. We failed, we learned, we keep digging until we have mastered it. We do so with respect, with patience, with determination, with kindness.

"Doubt is the biggest bluff in Life."
Dr. Bak Nguyen

Together we can change the world, a smile, a word, a hug at a time. We believe that spreading our hope and our joy, we can prevent diseases, depression, and suicide.

There is always hope, you just need to believe and be open. Remember that doubt is nothing but a big bluff.

"But if you let Doubt into your head, it will go down to your heart, and the bluff will become the truth."
Jonas Diop

You are in power, you have the power, the power to choose your reality, and to face its consequences. You are what you believe. You'll be what you feel.

Choose wisely what you let into your head, and even more carefully what you let into your heart. Stop talking about the **Big League**, we are talking about the **Impact League**.

One of my huge inspirations in life is Princess Diana. She used her status to end wars, to bring awareness to people all around the world, to help those in need.

She was beyond the monarchy, being a royalty from the size of her heart, not her crown. Just like Princess Diana, Dr. Bak's humility and kindness touched me.

Those people we talk about even when they are not around, even if they have past decades and centuries ago, those heroes we wrote in legends, well, they all saw the **beauty of Humanity**. They know that we are all related and that the good you are spreading will come around.

"When you help someone, anyone,
you are also helping yourself."
Jonas Diop

Are you ready to be the best human that you can be? You are a beautiful soul, I'll send you some praises. I love you as human, all of you. I love, and I hope. You?

This is **MASTERMIND, 7 ways into the big league.** Welcome to **MILLION DOLLAR MINDSET**.

One decision can turn your life around, you just need to take it.

JONAS DIOP

CONCLUSION

by Dr. BAK NGUYEN

Well, this is surely a surprise, a great one I must add. I always believe in Jonas and his potential. When I proposed to him to join me in the book, he was moved to see his name next to mine on the cover.

Yes, the cover is usually the first I do when I deduce to launch a new book… which is now every two weeks. I did so to encourage him as he finally finished the writing of his first opus, **NOW OR NEVER**.

We would have fun writing and exploring the concepts and the philosophies together. I knew that he could do it, I never had a doubt. But the real challenge is to keep up with me, writing at a frenetic pace while keep moving on in our daily lives.

That would prove to be the real challenge. I knew it, but I underestimate the impact that it would have on Jonas.

I took my precaution and played both our strengths, pushing him to post online a video in which we both appear and announcing to our audience this crazy challenge, crazy for him, another walk for me.

Of course, I wanted another book to keep my **Momentum** going, but I was looking to reward Jonas with a taste of the **power of Momentum**, now that he just finished his first book. To do so, I needed to show him a new way to write, another way to experience the challenge.

You see, Jonas is a proud man and a man of his word. He will promise you something and die doing it. Well, you don't need to die to prove a point. You can surf and have fun and still beat all the expectations!

That's what I wanted him to experiment while writing with me. This book was an excuse to have him try on a new lesson.

In the meantime, you did not lose your time either, as you have direct and almost unfiltered access to my mindset and the way I de-construct and assemble the world surrounding us.

The first lesson he learned was literal: by helping you to grow, he pressed me with specific questions. Since Jonas excels at his art, podcasting, he then empowering my world and teaching, giving them a second life, one that some times resonate louder than in my own draft.

Jonas mentioned that we are friends. He met me while I was saying **YES** to virtually everything and anything. Many people passed by, but Jonas is among the few I kept as a friend I can have fun with and keep evolving, increasing my already frenetic pace.

If he found a place in my entourage, it was mainly because of his loyalty, his curiosity and his tenacity to see things through. During the last two years, I saw him grinned, I saw him triumphed, I saw him destroyed. But after a few nights' sleep, he was back up, ready for more. Always smiling and respectful.

This is how he found a place in my team. But Jonas is not an employee, he is an officer that has the potential to blow things out of the water. This book is one of them.

You all know how fast and inspired I can be. Well, I surpassed my usual writing **MASTERMIND, 7 ways into the big league**, because I had someone to pitch me with questions, smart questions. Then, he shadowed me in my own game, challenging me to write 4 chapters within the first 3 days. Which I did.

I loved the vibe and the game. By the end of the 4th day, I was done writing my part. Now, it was for him to catch up. Well, by the 5th day, a day and a half before the expiration of our challenge, he hasn't sent me anything yet.

I went online and put pressure on him, the way Dr. Bak knows how, with respect, with style and with a lot of fun. A day before the conclusion of our book, I was starting to foresee that I will have to redo the cover without his name on it. I promised to deliver on November 1st, and the book will be available or, at least, submitted to Apple for that date.

Well, what happened next surprised me to my core. He not only delivered one chapter after the next, writing in a foreign language, but he beat me at my own game! He wrote the entirety of his part within 48 hours.

He had the support and my empowerment, but even inspired, I won't be writing as much, as fast raising up the level of quality and of content. Well, he got better, chapter after chapter.

He was fluid by the third one. I called him to congratulate him on the matter. I wanted him to experience and to feel the power of **Momentum**, which he did.

He achieved so because he trusted me and never gave up, even when everyone thought it might not be possible anymore! Congratulations Jonas, I am proud of you!

But we talked about cheating, how would I cheat in this situation. If 48 hours were not enough for me to deliver my part of the book, I would keep be pushing the boundaries until I reach the deadline. Then, just like any artist, I will submit what I have in hand.

The deadline will have pushed me to surpass myself, who cares if I miss the deadline? I do, but, well, better luck next time! I will keep writing with the same sense of urgency to complete my task. Even with a day late,

I will have completed my task and could go to another one.

That's the key, to finish, and to move forward to the next one, keeping only what is useful, what I can leverage on. A bad experience or the idea that I have given up will never be a great start for the next chapter.

So here is my advice, whatever challenge you take, give yourself less time to achieve it. Then, if you can deliver in your own timeframe, you may have a world record or at least a personal one. Even if you are late and miss your own delay, you will still be a winner to the rest of the world.

Is winning that important? If you read this book and understood that your powers lay within your emotions.

"What you feel and how you see yourself
is the key to your success."
Dr. Bak Nguyen

Jonas started with excitement as we began the project. Then as my chapter came in, he experienced intimidation and froze for a moment. He was behind, and he knew it.

By the 5th day, he could simply write me an email saying that he has too much on his plate, but he decided to show up in person instead. I respect that kind of courage to make your choice and to face its consequences.

I wasn't mad, I was impressed by his attitude. But we still have to deliver. So I made time in my crazy schedule to sit down with him and to show him how I would approach it, two days before the end.

He took in the advice and leverage on both my teaching and his stress. It is now 4 PM, Eastern time, November 1st. Since we are submitting to Apple, which operates on the West Coast, we still have 3 hours to cheat from…

I am waiting for his last chapter to come in to wrap this amazing project, **MASTERMIND, 7 ways into the big league**. More than a testimonial or a rhetorical book, you all had access to real and genuine information and secrets.

I gave you more than I originally planned. With the **Energy formula**, you have the key to your next level, whatever it is. But above all, you have witnessed how a man with potential and struggling to break free of his habits could make it into the big league.

Just like Jonas starting this book with, knowledge won't get you anywhere without actions. He took his steps and walked the path. Today, he felt the wind on his face and loved the feeling. How about you? Are you ready to trust in you and to bet on you?

I am. Follow those steps. Read the book a second time if you must, and just like Jonas, take action. Start small and grow each day, day after day.

"Discipline will breakdown mountains.
A rock at a time."
Dr. Bak Nguyen

Do so with **kindness**, with **respect**, with **gratitude**. That's the only way to obtain the help you need and to fill out the void you don't even know you had.

We all received the **gift of Life**. Since the Universe is Life, and Life runs in our veins, the power of the Universe is within each of us. You must only be quiet and aware enough to know what you are made of and to trust that inner voice.

Whatever talent or skill you've received, you'll also receive the **Gift of Time** to master, polish, and leverage on them. That's the real values, the real journey, the real potential.

May you find yourself and love the journey ahead. Oh, and by the way, this book will be submitted to Apple Book before the end of November 1st!

This is **MASTERMIND, 7 ways into the big league.** Welcome to **MILLION DOLLAR MINDSET**.

I am what I will, and I'll be what I tried.

Dr. BAK NGUYEN

EAX

ENHANCED AUDIO EXPERIENCE

A new way to learn and enjoy Audiobooks. Made to be entertaining while keeping the self-educational value of a book, EAX will appeal to both auditive and visual people. EAX is the blockbuster of the Audiobooks.

EAX will cover most of Dr. Bak's books, and is now negotiating to bring more authors and more titles to the EAX concept.

Now streaming on Spotify, Apple Music and available for download on all major music platforms. Give it a try today!

EAX

TOTAL IMMERSION WITH ENHANCED AUDIO EXPERIENCE

Streaming Audiobook Blockbuster

Search for Dr. Bak Nguyen on SPOTIFY, Apple Music and all major music platforms

FROM THE SAME AUTHOR
Dr. Bak Nguyen

www.DrBakNguyen.com

MAJOR LEAGUES' ACCESS

FACTEUR HUMAIN
LE LEADERSHIP DU SUCCÈS
par DR BAK NGUYEN & CHRISTIAN TRUDEAU

ehappyPedia
THE RISE OF THE UNICORN
BY DR. BAK NGUYEN & DR. JEAN DE SERRES

CHAMPION MINDSET
LEARNING TO WIN
BY DR. BAK NGUYEN & CHRISTOPHE MULUMBA

BRANDING DR.BAK
BALANCING STRATEGY AND EMOTIONS
BY DR. BAK NGUYEN, BRENDA GARCIA & SANTIAGO CHICA

BUSINESS

La Symphonie des Sens
ENTREPREUNARIAT
par DR BAK NGUYEN

Industries Disruptors
BY DR. BAK NGUYEN, ROUBA SAKR AND COLLABORATORS

Changing the World from a dental chair
BY DR. BAK NGUYEN

The Power Behind the Alpha
BY TRANIE VO & DR. BAK NGUYEN

SELFMADE
GRATITUDE AND HUMILITY
BY DR. BAK NGUYEN

CHILDREN'S BOOK
with William Bak

The Trilogy of Legends

THE LEGEND OF THE CHICKEN HEART
BY DR. BAK NGUYEN & WILLIAM BAK

THE LEGEND OF THE LION HEART
BY DR. BAK NGUYEN & WILLIAM BAK

THE LEGEND OF THE DRAGON HEART
BY DR. BAK NGUYEN & WILLIAM BAK

WE ARE ALL DRAGONS
BY DR. BAK NGUYEN & WILLIAM BAK

THE 9 SECRETS OF THE SMART CHICKEN
BY DR. BAK NGUYEN & WILLIAM BAK

THE SECRET OF THE FAST CHICKEN
BY DR. BAK NGUYEN & WILLIAM BAK

THE LEGEND OF THE SUPER CHICKEN
BY DR. BAK NGUYEN & WILLIAM BAK

THE STORY OF THE CHICKEN SHIT
BY DR. BAK NGUYEN & WILLIAM BAK

WHY CHICKEN CAN'T DREAM?
BY DR. BAK NGUYEN & WILLIAM BAK

THE STORY OF THE CHICKEN NUGGET
BY DR. BAK NGUYEN & WILLIAM BAK

LEGENDARY

IDENTITY
THE ANTHOLOGY OF QUESTS
BY DR. BAK NGUYEN

HYBRID
THE MODERN QUEST OF IDENTITY
BY DR. BAK NGUYEN

FORCES OF NATURE
FORGING THE CHARACTER OF WINNERS
BY DR. BAK NGUYEN

LIFESTYLE

HORIZON, BUILDING UP THE VISION
VOLUME ONE
BY DR. BAK NGUYEN

HORIZON, ON THE FOOTSTEP OF TITANS
VOLUME TWO
BY DR. BAK NGUYEN

MILLION DOLLAR MINDSET

MOMENTUM TRANSFER
BY DR. BAK NGUYEN & Coach DINO MASSON

LEVERAGE
COMMUNICATION INTO SUCCESS
BY DR. BAK NGUYEN AND COLLABORATORS

THE POWER OF YES
MY 18 MONTHS JOURNEY
BY DR. BAK NGUYEN

HOW TO WRITE A BOOK IN 30 DAYS
BY DR. BAK NGUYEN

POWER
EMOTIONAL INTELLIGENCE
BY DR. BAK NGUYEN

MENTORS
BY DR. BAK NGUYEN

HOW TO NOT FAIL AS A DENTIST
BY DR. BAK NGUYEN

HOW TO WRITE A SUCCESSFUL BUSINESS PLAN
BY DR. BAK NGUYEN & ROUBA SAKR

PARENTING

THE BOOK OF LEGENDS
BY DR. BAK NGUYEN & WILLIAM BAK

THE BOOK OF LEGENDS 2
BY DR. BAK NGUYEN & WILLIAM BAK

PERSONAL GROWTH

REBOOT
MIDLIFE CRISIS
BY DR. BAK NGUYEN

PHILOSOPHY

LEADERSHIP
PANDORA'S BOX
BY DR. BAK NGUYEN

KRYPTO
TO SAVE THE WORLD
BY DR. BAK NGUYEN & ILYAS BAKOUCH

DR.

Bak Nguyen

TITLES AVAILABLE AT

www.DrBakNguyen.com